# MATH AND SCIENCE INVESTIGATIONS

## HELPING YOUNG LEARNERS MAKE BIG DISCOVERIES

BY SALLY ANDERSON WITH THE
VERMONT CENTER FOR THE BOOK

## ALSO BY SALLY ANDERSON AND THE VERMONT CENTER FOR THE BOOK:

*Social Studies & Me: Using Children's Books to Learn about Our World*

*How Many Ways Can You Make Five? A Parent's Guide to Exploring Math with Children's Books*

*Where Does My Shadow Sleep? A Parent's Guide to Exploring Science with Children's Books*

GH10033
A Gryphon House Book

Early Childhood Education

A MOTHER GOOSE PROGRAM

# MATH and SCIENCE
# *Investigations*

**Helping Young Learners Make Big Discoveries**

**Sally Anderson**

**and *The Vermont Center for the Book***

**Gryphon House, Inc.**
Lewisville, NC

Published by Gryphon House, Inc.
PO Box 10, Lewisville, NC 27023
800.638.0928 (toll-free); 877.638.7576 (fax)

Visit us on the web at www.gryphonhouse.com

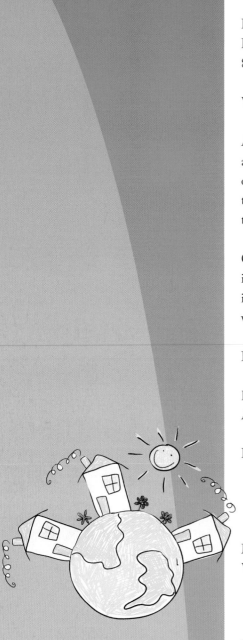

Interior illustrations by Mary Rojas and iStock LP.

**Library of Congress Cataloging-in-Publication Data**
Anderson, Sally.
  Math and science investigations : helping young learners make big discoveries/ By Sally Anderson and the Vermont Center for the Book.
     pages cm
  Includes bibliographical references and indexes.
  ISBN 978-0-87659-388-2
  1. Science--Study and teaching (Early childhood)--Activity programs. 2. Mathematics--Study and teaching (Early childhood)--Activity programs.  I. Vermont Center for the Book, issuing body. II. Title.
  LB1139.5.S3A53 2012
  372.35--dc23
                                        2012004492

**Bulk Purchase**
Gryphon House books are available for special premiums and sales promotions as well as for fund-raising use. Special editions or book excerpts also can be created to specifications. For details, contact the Director of Marketing at Gryphon House.

**Disclaimer**
Gryphon House, Inc. and the author cannot be held responsible for damage, mishap, or injury incurred during the use of or because of activities in this book. Appropriate and reasonable caution and adult supervision of children involved in activities and corresponding to the age and capability of each child involved is recommended at all times. Do not leave children unattended at any time. Observe safety and caution at all times.

# TABLE OF CONTENTS

## CHAPTER 1

# Introduction

## WELCOME TO *MATH AND SCIENCE INVESTIGATIONS*

This book will support and enhance the work you are already doing with young children. In it you will find hundreds of ideas for using high-quality picture books, good conversations, and lively investigations that incorporate the skills, concepts, and standards of mathematics, science, and language and literacy.

In addition, this book will help you work with children in ways that are interesting and fun to them and sensitive to their developmental needs.

Children are naturally compelled to explore the world around them. By providing tools and support for children's active exploration, you can promote the development of mathematics, science, and language and literacy learning. By observing and documenting this learning, you can share with administrators, peers, and families the learning that is taking place within each child.

*Math and Science Investigations* will enhance your work with young children by helping you to:

O Use the language of math, science, and literacy in your daily practice and programming,

O Use picture books and investigations to promote conversations, language skills, and higher-order thinking,

○ Engage children in hands-on investigations that help them explore math, science, and literacy skills and concepts,

○ Find diverse ways to use picture books for all kinds of learning,

○ Learn how to use math, science, and language and literacy standards to inform your work with children,

○ Observe individual children and groups of children more carefully,

○ Learn ways to communicate to families the work you are doing with children,

○ Enjoy your time with children and continue to grow in your profession, and

○ Understand that you enrich the lives of young children.

Using *Math and Science Investigations* will help you work with children with more intention, talk about your work with more clarity, and address standards more thoroughly. *Math and Science Investigations* will help you build on what you already know about mathematics, science, and language and literacy.

## HOW THIS BOOK IS ORGANIZED

Each remaining chapter of *Math and Science Investigations* focuses on a topic that relates to both mathematics and science. The chapters are as follows:

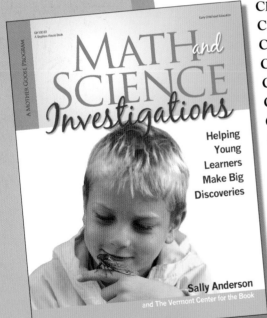

**Chapter 2: Measurement, Data Collection, and Graphic Representation**
**Chapter 3: More Than Counting**
**Chapter 4: Out and About**
**Chapter 5: Shapes and Spaces**
**Chapter 6: Exploring Spaces (and Places!)**
**Chapter 7: What Comes Next?**
**Chapter 8: Growing and Changing**
**Chapter 9: Same and Different**
**Chapter 10: Making It Work**

Each chapter begins with a general introduction to the theme: ideas to start you thinking about math, science, and language and literacy; vocabulary related to the topic; and picture book suggestions. The introduction also answers these important questions:

○ How does the theme respond to young children's curiosity and interest?

○ How does the theme relate to young children's development?

○ How does the theme relate to math, science, and literacy?

## INVESTIGATIONS

The introduction to the theme is followed by two or more investigations. Investigations are experiences that engage children in math, science, and language and literacy learning. Investigations are meaningful learning experiences that are done over and over again. They are child-centered, they build children's self-confidence, and they deepen children's understanding of skills and concepts.

Each investigation begins with a summary of what children will do and learn during the investigation. Most also offer picture-book suggestions. Investigations are divided into these subsections:

What's Needed: Materials needed to do the investigation.

Things to Consider: What you'll want to think about before beginning the investigation.

Key Standards Children Practice: Standards highlighted in this investigation.

Step by Step: How the investigation should proceed.

Talk with Children: Open-ended questions and comments to stimulate children's language and thinking during the investigation.

Observe Children: Questions to ask yourself about children's language and behaviors as you observe children during the investigation.

Extend the Learning: Ways to deepen and extend the investigation to enrich children's math and science learning.

Connect with Families: Information to display and post about children's learning during investigations.

The chapters and investigations are not cumulative. Pick and choose individual investigations or a series of investigations that can be easily integrated into your curriculum, that address the children's interests, or that explore an event that a child or the class experienced. Keep in mind that all books, conversations, and investigations can be repeated.

# WHY USE PICTURE BOOKS TO INTRODUCE MATH AND SCIENCE?

Stories are a powerful way to introduce math and science to children. Researchers recommend using picture books to develop math and science skills and understanding because picture books:

- Provide a story context for math and science content;
- Suggest manipulatives for a variety of math and science investigations;
- Pose problems that can be explored using varied strategies;
- Develop math and science concepts;
- Encourage the use of math and science language;
- Modify story situations to develop math and science thinking;
- Introduce new vocabulary;
- Enhance phonological awareness through repetitive patterns, rhymes, and refrains;
- Introduce complex sentence structures;
- Help children understand themselves and others;
- Help children make sense of their world; and
- Encourage children to recreate stories in their own words.

Stories bring math and science to life. They can help children learn how to use math or science skills and knowledge to address their own real-life problems as they arise. At the same time, children are developing critical language-development skills.

# THE IMPORTANCE OF A DIVERSE BOOK COLLECTION

When we recommend books in this guide, we have selected them to reflect the diversity of the world. This means that we look for good, well-reviewed picture books that strike a balance of gender, ethnicity, and place.

Diversity plays an important role in choosing and reading picture books, but we never isolate these books or categorize them according to the demographic they may reflect. Nor do we choose books simply because they represent a particular culture. Story, art, and publishing excellence are always the primary criteria. In all books recommended in this Guide, the characters share the same needs and desires as the young children in your care: they want to explore the world and learn new things, they want to be loved, and they want to feel safe—but they want to have adventures, too.

### Using Nonfiction Books

In addition to using picture books to introduce a math or science idea, you may want to delve further into the facts by using nonfiction books. For instance, you could pair Chris Van Allsburg's *Two Bad Ants* with a good nonfiction book about ants.

Nonfiction books present facts and photographs or scaled drawings about a subject. Here are some things to consider when using nonfiction books:

O   Nonfiction books are not meant to be read aloud from cover to cover. Before you use a nonfiction book, read it from cover to cover as you would with a picture book. Choose the parts of the book that reinforce, extend, or otherwise add to the concept you and the children are exploring.

O   Give the children time to look closely at photographs and illustrations. Read the captions to them to help explain what they are looking at.

O   Stop reading after a few facts and talk about them.

O   Use the nonfiction book to compare and contrast with the picture book. Do the ants in the photo look like the two bad ants? How are they the same? How are they different?

## THE IMPORTANCE OF VOCABULARY DEVELOPMENT

The research is clear: the more words a child knows before he or she enters school, the more successful learning will take place for years to come. Reading is important, but complex conversation is key. In your everyday activities with children, use precise language as you ask questions or describe objects or events.

## INTRODUCING PICTURE BOOKS

Throughout *Math and Science Investigations* we have suggested picture books for you to use with the children. What follows are suggestions on how to introduce two picture books to children. Both *Lottie's New Beach Towel* by Petra Mathers and *Bein' with You This Way* by W. Nikola-Lisa are excellent picture books in their own right. However, embedded in both stories are simple math and science concepts.

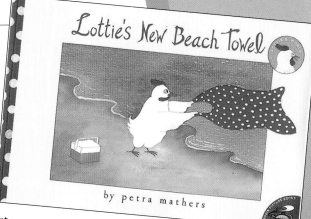

*Lottie's New Beach Towel*
Little does Lottie realize that the beautiful new beach towel her Aunt Mattie sent her will help her solve problems. After all, Lottie's just planning to enjoy a day at the beach with her good friend Herbie—what could go wrong? But when she first steps on the hot, hot sand, she confronts the first of several problems she'll use the beach towel to solve.

Lottie uses the same problem-solving skills that mathematicians and scientists use.

Introduction

### Vocabulary

*ingenuity:* cleverness. When children are clever at solving problems, use the word ingenuity to describe what they are doing.

*problem:* a difficult situation. This book is about solving problems. When we solve problems in our daily lives:

- We observe a situation,
- We raise questions,
- We make predictions and a plan,
- We try the plan, and if the plan doesn't work...
- We make a new plan, and
- We try that new plan.

## MAKING CONNECTIONS

Before you read *Lottie's New Beach Towel* with the children, show them the other books you've read together. Talk about the problems in the stories and how the problems were solved. You might start with these books:

*Bunny Cakes* by Rosemary Wells
*The Doorbell Rang* by Pat Hutchins
*Seven Blind Mic*e by Ed Young

For each of these, discuss how the problem was solved and what some other solutions might be.

## INTRODUCING THE BOOK

Begin reading *Lottie's New Beach Towel* by looking at the front cover and the endpapers together. Ask questions such as the following:

*What do you notice about the cover?*
*What do you notice about the endpapers?*
*What does the front cover tell us about the book?*
*Can you learn anything new from the back cover?*

Next, look at the picture of the opened package on the title page.
Make sure to read what is on the address label and talk about it—some children may not know that what's printed on a package tells where it should be delivered. Then tell the children they're going to observe carefully and make a prediction. Ask questions such as the following:

*What do you see in the picture?*
*What do you think will happen in the story?*

MATH AND SCIENCE INVESTIGATIONS

## READING AND TALKING TOGETHER

Read *Lottie's New Beach Towel* with as few interruptions as possible so that the children understand the story. After reading the book several times, act it out with the children. Use props in the classroom such as a blanket for a beach towel and retell the story. Let the children take turns being Lottie, Herbie, and the other characters.

*Lottie's New Beach Towel* provides a wonderful opportunity to talk about problems and solutions long after you've read the book with children. When a child has a problem—for example, not being able to find something—take the time to point out that this is a problem to be solved. It can be solved by taking specific actions, and there may be more than one solution to the problem. Ask questions such as the following:

*What is the problem?*
*What are some ways it might be solved?*
*Which way will you try first?*

Pair *Lottie's New Beach Towel* with investigations such as "What Would You Do If...?" on page 158 and "How Does It Help Us?" on page 161 in the Making It Work chapter. Lottie's problem is a great jumping-off point to math and science investigations focusing on problem solving.

In *Bein' with You This Way*, a young girl leads a cumulative rap about individual differences. The playground is a perfect setting for this exuberant story.

This original verse has a challenging and inviting beat. The wonderful, rhythmic chant is about all the ways people are the same and different. Make sure you practice reading *Bein' with You This Way* aloud before you read it to children.

### Vocabulary

*electrifying:* exciting or stimulating. Vocabulary building can be part of conversation. When a child has a good idea or paints a bright picture, say: "Now, that is simply electrifying!"
*enraptured:* filled with delight. Children are enraptured by a good story well told.

## MAKING CONNECTIONS

Before reading *Bein' with You This Way* to children, ask your group to look at what the children are wearing on their feet. Some are probably wearing sneakers and some are not. *I'm going to sort our entire group into two different groups.*

Now sort the children by putting (without telling them why!) the "sneakered" children in one group and the "sneakerless" children in another. *Can anybody figure out what attribute I used to sort you?*

Do this several times, using different attributes. Always give the children plenty of opportunities to discuss what they think the attributes are. Encourage the children to use good descriptive words. Older children may want to choose attributes and do the sorting themselves. Sorting options are endless, but do not sort children by physical characteristics.

## INTRODUCING THE BOOK

Show the children the cover of the book. Notice that the picture on the front cover extends to the back cover. Talk with your group about feelings, the weather, and the location when looking at the cover.
*What do you notice about the playground?*
*What do you notice about the children?*

Look at the title page of the book together. Ask:
*What do you notice about this group of children?*

## READING AND TALKING TOGETHER

After you've read *Bein' with You This Way* a few times, encourage the children to participate in this call-and-response story. Pause and invite children to say "Uh-huh!," "Mm-mmm," and "Ah-ha!"

○ Engage the children in a conversation about same and different. Here are some questions you might ask:
*How is this red marker the same as this red toy car? How is it different?*
*How is a flashlight the same as a lamp? How is it different?*
*How is a dog the same as a person? How is it different?*
*How is a bicycle the same as a car? How is it different?*

○ Go on a "Same and Different" hunt. Allow the children plenty of time to find two objects that they think are the same and different.

Come back together and have the children talk about what is the same and what is different about the objects they found. Some children may want to talk about objects that cannot be easily moved, such as a window and a mirror. Encourage the children to point to these objects and talk about them to the group.

You might continue this investigation outdoors. Tell the children to use their observation skills to look for objects (living and nonliving) that are the same and different.

Pair *Bein' with You This Way* with investigations such as "What's the Rule?" on page 144 in the Same and Different chapter of this book.

## HOW YOUNG CHILDREN LEARN

Young children learn through exploration. Children explore in hundreds of different ways. For young children, learning takes place everywhere and all the time. You can observe children exploring when they do the following:

- **Repeat actions over and over:** Chloe works on the same puzzle over and over.
- **Lift things up and look underneath:** Olivia turns over the rocks in the park.
- **Ask questions:** Isabella asks, "Why does the fish make bubbles?"
- **Use materials and tools in creative ways:** Juan uses a piece of rope to measure a tower of blocks.
- **Watch things intently:** Mia likes to watch the hamster running around and around on its wheel.
- **Make predictions:** Noah guesses that a raccoon might live in a hollow log.
- **Solve problems:** Maria substitutes two small blocks for one bigger one.
- **Represent real objects:** Jayden draws two parallel lines, connects them, and says, "It's a train track!"
- **Make comparisons:** Ethan uses the small blanket to wrap up the smaller of two dolls and a bigger blanket to wrap up the larger doll.
- **Sort objects:** Jacob separates a collection of buttons into two groups: metal ones and plastic ones.
- **Make connections:** Emma tells some friends to make playdough pies that look like the pies in a book they listened to at story time.

It is not difficult to become an effective math and science teacher for young children. Chances are good that you and your children are already doing many science- and math-related activities as you go about your day. Here are ways to encourage mathematics and science learning in everyday situations:

- Setting the table for lunch is a chance to count and create a pattern with the napkins, utensils, and dishes.
- Going outside to play means being able to observe and talk about plants, the sun, shadows, wind, or gravity, just to list a few possibilities.
- Watching the fish in the aquarium or the hamster in its cage provides a wonderful opportunity for comparing and contrasting two different living things.
- Cooking up a batch of cookies requires counting, measuring, combining solids and liquids, and using all of the senses!
- When it's time to go home at the end of a busy day, children can recall the sequence of the day and predict what tomorrow might bring.

This book will help you (and the children with whom you work) become more aware of and purposeful about the math and science that you do every day. You will find yourself talking about these skills, using the appropriate vocabulary, and having fun exploring other ways to do routine activities!

The investigations presented in this book support children's learning by engaging them in three important components of learning: actions, conversations, and thinking.

## MATH, SCIENCE, AND LANGUAGE AND LITERACY STANDARDS

Standards help educators bring focus and intention to their work with children. This book emphasizes both content (knowledge and ideas) and process skills (behaviors and thinking) in the mathematics, science, and language and literacy areas.

More and more, educators are being asked to learn about standards and incorporate them into their work with children. When used appropriately, standards have a positive effect on children's learning. Standards are designed to answer these questions:

O  What should children learn?
O  When should they learn it?
O  What outcomes can be expected?

Keep in mind that for young children, we want to create learning environments that encourage reaching toward these kinds of ideas.

Professional organizations such as the National Council of Teachers of Mathematics (NCTM), The National Academy of Science (NAS), and the National Council of Teachers of English (NCTE), as well as most state departments of education, have created and published sets of standards for a range of age and grade levels. State and local standards can be easily accessed on the Internet.

The following pages detail early childhood standards for mathematics, science, and language and literacy. They are defined in a way you will find meaningful and useful in your work with young children. You can easily make connections between these standards and your own state or local standards and the Head Start Framework of Outcomes.

As you become familiar with these three sets of standards, you will notice that they overlap and interconnect. This is the nature of learning—it doesn't fall into neat little separate bundles. Math skills help us with science, science skills help us with math, and language and literacy skills help us in all areas.

# MATHEMATICS STANDARDS

In Principles and Standards for School Mathematics, the NCTM sets forth standards in 10 areas that cover a broad range of math skills and understandings—five are identified as process standards and five as content standards.

## THE PROCESS STANDARDS

Learning mathematics requires action and thinking. NCTM has identified five processes that are especially critical to learning about mathematics: problem solving, reasoning and proof, communicating, making connections, and representing.

## Problem Solving

| For young children, this includes the following: |
| --- |
| • Using simple approaches to solving mathematical problems: asking for help, counting, trial-and-error, guessing-and-checking. |

## Reasoning and Proof

| For young children, this includes the following: |
| --- |
| • Learning to explain how they solved a mathematical problem: describing the steps taken verbally, in a drawing or with concrete objects. |

## Communicating

| For young children, this includes the following: |
| --- |
| • Telling others about their math-related work: using language, pictures or other symbols, or concrete objects; and |
| • Beginning to use some math language: numbers, shape names, size words, names of math materials, and so on. |

## Making Connections

| For young children, this includes the following: |
| --- |
| • Using math skills in a variety of situations, not just when prompted by an adult; |
| • Linking their own math experiences to those of other people, in real life or in books; and |
| • Recalling previous math experiences when engaged in current ones. |

## Representing

| For young children, this includes the following: |
| --- |
| • Using simple pictures, graphs, diagrams, or dictated words to represent their mathematical ideas. |

## The Content Standards

### Numbers and Operations

| For young children, this includes the following: |
| --- |
| • Recognizing and naming some written numerals; |
| • Having a sense of quantity: knowing that the number name "three" and the symbol "3" mean three of something; |
| • Counting: learning the sequence of number names (1, 2, 3); |
| • Counting objects: learning to count an object only once, using one-to-one correspondence in counting objects and matching groups of objects; |
| • Beginning addition: adding two groups of concrete objects by counting the total; |
| • Beginning subtraction: taking away one group of concrete objects from another by taking some away and counting the remainder; and |
| • Comparing: understanding ideas such as more than, less than, and the same as and having a general idea that some numbers stand for a lot and some numbers mean a little. |

### Geometry and Spatial Sense

| For young children, this includes the following: |
| --- |
| • Matching, sorting, naming, and describing shapes: circles, squares, rectangles, and triangles; |
| • Naming and describing shapes found in everyday environments; |
| • Combining shapes to make new shapes; |
| • Making shape designs that have symmetry and balance; and |
| • Understanding and using words that describe where objects are located: *over, under, through, above, below, beside, behind, near, far, inside, outside.* |

### Patterns, Functions, and Algebra

| For young children, this includes the following: |
| --- |
| • Identifying, copying, and making simple patterns: sequenced or repeated organization of objects, sounds, or events; |
| • Using patterns to predict what will come next in a sequence; |
| • Recognizing single number patterns such as "one more"; and |
| • Noticing, describing, and explaining mathematical changes in quantity, size, temperature, or weight. |

## Measurement

| For young children, this includes the following: |
| --- |
| • Understanding and using words referring to quantities: *big, little, tall, short, long, a lot, a little, hot, cold, heavy, light*; |
| • Understanding and using comparative words: *more than, less than, bigger than, smaller than, shorter than, longer than, heavier than, colder than*; |
| • Showing an awareness of and interest in measuring: imitating the use of measuring tools and measuring with nonstandard units; |
| • Comparing objects such as "Which of two sticks is longer?"; and |
| • Beginning to use measurement words, such as *inches, feet, miles, pounds, minutes,* and *hours* in their language. |

## Data Analysis, Statistics, and Probability

| For young children, this includes the following: |
| --- |
| • Sorting objects to answer questions; |
| • Collecting data to answer a question: keeping track of simple information gathered from a group of people or over a short length of time; and |
| • Making lists or basic graphs, with (adult) help, to organize collected data. |

# EXPLORING MATHEMATICS

In your everyday work with children, try to identify math skills, processes, and concepts that are developmentally appropriate. Weave the math concepts into learning centers, investigations, and book reading...

### ...by talking

In everyday conversation, use appropriate mathematics vocabulary such as sequence, solution, shape names, positional words, directional words.

O

Talk about the math in everyday situations: measuring, counting, problem solving, pattern recognition, the position of things, sequences, and transitions.

O

Wonder aloud about numbers of things, comparisons, problems, and solutions.

O

Look for and talk about numbers everywhere: on clocks, radios, clothing, appliances, signs, houses.

O

Brainstorm solutions to everyday problems.

O

Encourage children to use directions and positional language.

### ...by investigating

Provide materials that encourage mathematics explorations: shapes, blocks, collections of small objects, items to fill and empty.

○

Use concrete objects for counting, comparing, measuring, sorting.

○

Use everyday situations in indoor and outdoor environments to promote mathematics learning.

○

Create patterns of objects, colors, shapes, and words.

○

Look for and describe patterns in the indoor and outdoor environments: on book jackets, clothing, in a garden, on buildings.

○

Make counting books.

### ...with books

Borrow or buy books that have explicit math content: counting, measuring, and so on.

○

Read books that have repeated sequences of events, point out the events, and give children an opportunity to make predictions—"What happens next?"

○

Look for math words and concepts in all picture books.

○

Make connections between shapes in books and shapes in the environment.

○

Talk about the problems book characters are solving. Brainstorm other suggestions for solving those problems.

### ...with tools and technology

Have balances and standard and nonstandard measuring tools available.

○

Obtain computer programs that allow children to explore mathematics concepts.

### ...through documentation

Display graphs and charts to help children compare numbers and other mathematical thinking.

○

Encourage children to represent their mathematical thinking with drawings and other projects.

○

Record the outdoor temperature daily. When discussing the data, use words such as *colder than, warmer than,* and *the same as.*

○

Help children make drawings, charts, books, and models of their math investigations.

### ...by supporting mathematics in the home

Make families aware of their children's interests, skills, and abilities.

○

Share books with specific math content: counting, shape, and sorting books.

○

Let families know that math is everywhere in the home environment.

○

Share simple math activities with families.

# SCIENCE STANDARDS

In the National Science Education Standards, the National Research Council sets forth standards in eight areas that cover a broad range of science skills and understanding for children in kindergarten through grade 12. These standards have been adapted to apply to young children. Science as Inquiry, Physical Science, Life Science, Earth and Space Science, and Design Technology are addressed in this book. Not included are Science in Personal and Social Perspectives and the History and Nature of Science.

## SCIENCE AS INQUIRY

The process skills of science are the Science as Inquiry standard, listed below in alphabetical order. Children need to practice the process skills of science so that they learn to ask questions about the world and then study the world in special ways to find answers, just like scientists do.

Young children learn science by doing science. Young children need experiences that allow them to explore, over and over. They need to use a variety of materials and tools, talk about what they are doing, ask questions, and try to find answers.

Science as Inquiry includes the following:

## Asking Scientific Questions

| For young children, this includes the following: |
|---|
| • Questions such as: *What's that?, How did it happen?, What if...?* and *How many?* |

## Collecting and Using Data

| For young children, this includes the following: |
|---|
| • Thinking back on what they have observed, sorted, or measured, in order to explain their ideas about the world around them. |

## Communicating Information and Ideas

| For young children, this includes the following: |
|---|
| • Using conversations, drawings, and/or simple charts to tell others about what they have learned and to offer explanations, even though they might not be scientifically accurate. |

## Designing and Making Models

| For young children, this includes the following: |
|---|
| • Planning and creating models, and |
| • Building from plans. |

## Estimating and Predicting

**For young children, this includes the following:**

• Using clues to make informed guesses about quantities, causes and effects, or unknown information.

## Experimenting

**For young children, this includes the following:**

• Pursuing answers to questions through controlled investigations.

## Finding Patterns

**For young children, this includes the following:**

• Noticing repeated sequences and organized arrangements in the world, seeing and understanding how one thing influences another.

## Measuring

**For young children, this includes the following:**

• Making comparisons of sizes, temperatures, and weights, as well as using numbers to quantify measurement. For young children, measurement can rely on nonstandard units of measurement such as spoons, straws, shoes, and other material in the environment, not just feet and inches.

## Noticing Change over Time

**For young children, this includes the following:**

• Recognizing and describing how objects and living things change—either quickly (an ice cube melting) or more slowly (a plant growing).

## Observing

**For young children, this includes the following:**

• Using our senses to explore and learn about scientific objects and events.

## Recognizing Relationships

**For young children, this includes the following:**

• Comparing sizes, shapes, quantities, colors, and events.

## Sorting and Classifying

**For young children, this includes the following:**

• Noticing similarities and differences and putting objects into groups based on shared attributes (characteristics).

MATH AND SCIENCE INVESTIGATIONS

## Using Simple Tools of Science

**For young children, this includes the following:**

- Using tools, such as magnifiers, eyedroppers, water pumps, balances, sieves, and binoculars to explore and investigate.

## DESIGN TECHNOLOGY

Young children are always making things. Design Technology is about the many ways people, and now computers, have designed tools, machines, and other inventions to solve problems big and small. Young children are naturally interested in tools and machines; they want to try to use them, and they want to understand how the tools and machines work. Young children also enjoy using their imaginations to invent solutions to everyday problems.

Here are some ways children learn about Design Technology:

- Asking questions such as: *How can we build it? What is it made of? How can we change it?*
- Responding to What if? questions, such as: *What if someone had not invented a zipper? What would we do if we didn't have cars to get us from one place to another? What if there was no bridge over the water?*
- Taking apart a broken telephone or clock and naming the different pieces.
- Noticing a problem and coming up with possible changes in design.
- Using varied materials to build an imaginative invention and describing the problem it would solve.
- Examining a collection of kitchen or carpenter's tools and making guesses about what each one does.

## EARTH AND SPACE SCIENCE

Young children are interested in many different aspects of the land and sky that make up our world. As young children experience soil, sand, rocks, puddles, streams, ponds, rainbows, shadows, the moon, and stars in their everyday lives, they begin to notice characteristics, patterns, and changes related to these elements of earth and space. As young children gain knowledge about earth and space, they may also learn to respect and care for the environment.

Here are some ways children learn about Earth and Space Science:

- Noticing and describing similarities and differences between night and day, the seasons, and weather conditions.
- Collecting, describing, and weighing rocks, pebbles, soil, and/or sand.
- Investigating the shape, position, and change in shadows.
- Looking for "cloud pictures" in the sky and naming different types of clouds.
- Noticing and talking about the sun, moon, and stars.
- Sorting a collection of clothing, footwear, or objects according to seasons.
- Looking at a thermometer to decide whether or not to wear a jacket for outside play.
- Flying kites on windy and calm days.

## LIFE SCIENCE

Living things are a source of endless fascination for young children. When children observe and talk about a variety of living things, they learn about basic needs, ways of moving, life cycles, habitats, growth patterns, and the interdependence of living things.

Here are some ways children learn about Life Science:
- Measuring themselves and recording their own heights and weights.
- Planting seeds, watching them grow, and giving them sunlight, water, and plant food.
- Using a magnifying glass (or *hand lens*, the scientific name) to study worms, insects, or a flower.
- Collecting and sorting different types of leaves.
- Matching and sorting pictures of animals based on what they look like, where they live, or what they eat.

## PHYSICAL SCIENCE

As children explore the world around them, they learn about the properties of objects and materials—what they're made of, their size, shape, color, texture, weight, and temperature. They also learn about motion, sound, and light.

Children are fascinated by what happens to various objects in different situations: *Do the objects sink or float in water? Do they dissolve or disintegrate? What do we notice when water gets very hot or very cold?*

Here are some ways children learn about Physical Science:
- Collecting and examining objects such as rocks with a magnifying glass and sorting them into groups based on shape, color, or texture.
- Rolling, catching, bouncing, kicking, and throwing different kinds of balls.
- Making musical instruments out of materials such as cardboard tubes, tin plates, cans, and jar lids to explore sound in all its varieties.

# EXPLORING SCIENCE

In your everyday work with children, try to identify science concepts that are developmentally appropriate. Weave the science concepts into learning centers, investigations, and book reading.

### ...by talking

In everyday conversations use appropriate science vocabulary such as *observe, predict, estimate, count, experiment,* and *compare.*

○

Talk about natural phenomena: the weather, animal behaviors, plants, clouds, and so on.

○

Talk about characters from books who have problems and about how they solve the problems.

Wonder aloud and ask questions relating to current classroom activities: *Will we be able to see our shadows today?*

O

Encourage children to make estimations, predictions, and hypotheses.

O

Use proper vocabulary when talking about the world around you.

O

Allow plenty of time to discuss the investigations you are doing.

O

Talk about the questions children have about your indoor and outdoor environment.

O

Talk about the changes you notice in: the weather, each other, the seasons, your neighborhood.

O

Before transitions, ask: *What do you think will happen next?*

O

Look for patterns and sequences in everyday activities: After we have a snack, what happens next?

O

Ask questions about new experiences: How is this different? How is this the same?

O

Talk about the connections you see between and among different objects.

**...with books**

Borrow or buy books about science, including picture biographies of scientists and other reference books.

O

Look at a reference book of insects, animals, or trees noticing similarities and differences.

O

Provide books that show children information about environments, diversity, growth, shadows, and other scientific ideas.

O

Display books and science equipment in several places, not just in a science corner.

O

Make predictions about what will happen in stories.

O

Read game or other instructions aloud to children.

O

After reading a book about growing plants, plant some seeds.

O

Follow a recipe from a cookbook.

O

Play a game based on a story, such as Shadow Tag when you read a book about shadows.

**...with tools and technology**

Have magnifying glasses, balances, and other science equipment available.

O

Observe and talk about scientific and technological devices such as thermometers, calculators, and computers.

Measure objects with standard and nonstandard units.

Explore a tree trunk with a hand lens.

Compare the weights of different objects by hand; then use a balance to weigh them.

Look up a weather forecast on the Internet.

Use an eyedropper to mix colors.

Make shadows with a flashlight.

Check the temperature outside on cold and hot days.

Imagine together what life was like before telephones or television.

**...through documentation**

Have fun making charts and lists and display them.

Help children make drawings, models, and books about their investigations.

Describe and document changes that are taking place among the children, in the classroom, and in the outdoor environment.

Plant seeds, measure seedlings, and make drawings of the plants' growth at weekly intervals.

Visit a special tree periodically throughout the year and document differences and similarities.

**...by supporting science in the home**

Make families aware of their children's interests, skills, and abilities.

Publicize informal science opportunities in your community.

Invite families on field trips.

Make sure families know about the local science or children's museum.

Tell families about investigations their children really enjoy.

# LANGUAGE AND LITERACY STANDARDS

Many organizations have made significant contributions to our understanding of what constitutes the best in language and literacy education. They are the International Reading Association, the National Council of Teachers of English, the National Research Council's Committee on the Prevention of Reading Difficulties in Young Children, the National Association for the Education of Young Children, and the Common Core State Standards Initiative. We have combined and adapted the standards that follow.

## Language and Vocabulary Development

| For young children, this includes the following: |
| --- |
| • Taking part in meaningful conversations with adults about many different topics; |
| • Listening to and using all kinds of new words: *noun, verb, adjective, adverb*; |
| • Engaging in many different experiences in order to have interesting things to think and talk about; |
| • Singing songs, chanting rhymes, and doing fingerplays; and |
| • Listening to books that have stimulating language and vocabulary. |

## Phonological Awareness

| For young children, this includes the following: |
| --- |
| • Playing with the sounds of language through songs, rhymes, and chants; |
| • Playing with both real and nonsensical rhyming words; |
| • Hearing how some words have the same beginning sound (*Peter/peach*); and |
| • Hearing the difference between words that sound very similar (*boat/goat, witch/wish*). |

## Understanding Stories

| For young children, this includes the following: |
| --- |
| • Listening to stories read from books, told orally, told with puppets or as drama, and recorded on tapes or CDs; |
| • Sharing their own stories and experiences orally and through artwork; |
| • Talking about the characters in stories; and |
| • Recalling the sequence of simple stories. |

## Book Awareness

| For young children, this includes the following: |
| --- |
| • Knowing where books are kept, |
| • Handling books gently, |
| • Holding a book right-side-up, |
| • Opening the cover of the book first, and |
| • Becoming aware of the parts of a book (front and back covers, endpapers, title page, author, illustrator, dedication, and so on). |

## Book Exposure

| For young children, this includes the following: |
| --- |
| • Hearing a wide variety of books and stories: fiction, nonfiction, and poetry; and |
| • Hearing books and stories that reflect all types of diversity: racial, ethnic, language, socio-economic, ability, gender, age, religious, and geographic. |

## Comprehension

| For young children, this includes the following: |
| --- |
| • Understanding the meaning of language in everyday conversations and stories; |
| • Asking questions and making comments relevant to conversations and stories; |
| • Showing appropriate emotion during a story by looking sad or laughing; |
| • Relating information and events in conversations and stories to their own life experiences; |
| • Following who said or did what in conversations and stories; |
| • Identifying a favorite part of a story and telling why; |
| • Retelling stories by looking at illustrations, on a flannel board, with a puppet or stuffed animal, or through drama; |
| • Responding to questions about stories, both open-ended questions as well as who, what, when, where, why, and how questions; |
| • Memorizing some of the words from a story and finishing repetitive phrases or sentences; and |
| • Predicting what might happen next in a story. |

## Knowledge of Print

| For young children, this includes the following: |
| --- |
| • Understanding that print conveys different kinds of messages; |
| • Pointing to print from left to right and top to bottom as they pretend to read books; |
| • Asking adults to read or write signs, books, labels, and other forms of print; and |
| • Being aware that letters can be represented in different ways. |

## Letter and Word Awareness

| For young children, this includes the following: |
| --- |
| • Differentiating letters and print from pictorial, numerical, and graphic symbols; |
| • Singing or chanting along when the alphabet is sung or recited; |
| • Recognizing and/or naming some letters of the alphabet in their environment (on their cubbies, artwork, games, puzzles, signs); |
| • Recognizing their name and a few other key words in their environment; and |
| • Adding letter-like symbols and/or letters to their artwork, or making signs for block structures. |

## Literacy as a Source of Enjoyment

| For young children, this includes the following: |
| --- |
| • Choosing to look at books independently, |
| • Having favorite books and asking for them to be read repeatedly, and |
| • Getting excited about a trip to the library. |

# EXPLORING LANGUAGE AND LITERACY

In your everyday work with children, try to identify language and literacy concepts that are developmentally appropriate. Weave the language and literacy concepts into learning centers, investigations, and book reading...

**...by reading aloud**
Read aloud to children at least once a day.

Ο

Read to children in small groups and individually.

Ο

Encourage children to look carefully at the book itself: cover, endpapers, and title page.

Ο

Note the names of the author and illustrator and the dedication page.

Ο

Occasionally point out key features of print (left-to-right/top-to-bottom progression, spaces between words, punctuation).

Ο.

Take time to introduce a new book to children.

Ο

Choose books that reflect the diversity of our world.

Ο

Read different kinds of stories: nonfiction, fantasy, funny, sad, rhyming.

Ο

Get to know books before sharing them with children.
Sit so that all children are comfortable and can easily see the illustrations.

Ο

Be dramatic! Be silly—play with different voices, make funny or scary sounds, shout, whisper, pause dramatically or speed up when there's a lot of action, and slow down at the end of a book.

**Read the same book in different ways:**
• Straight through with as few interruptions as possible;
• "Read" the pictures instead of the words;
• Before reading a page, ask children to predict what might happen;
• Encourage children to say repeating phrases.

○

Reread the same book many times.

**...by talking**
Help children make connections between stories and their own experiences.

○

Build vocabulary by discussing one or two words that might be new to children.

○

Use the new words as often as possible.

**Engage in conversations about:**
• The story's setting—where it took place;
• The characters—what they did or said, what they are like;
• The sequence of events in the story—beginning, middle, end;
• The problem and solution in the story; and
• How the story makes children feel.

○

Find opportunities to talk about similarities and differences in words and sounds.

○

Let children supply missing rhyming words when reading rhyming stories and poems.

○

Engage children in retelling the story.

○

Talk about the books you are reading.

○

Refer to books in your conversations with children.

○

Have brief discussions when you reach the end of stories.

○

Ask children to tell about their favorite stories at circle or group time.

○

Help extend rather than direct children's conversations.

**...through activities**
Engage children in activities related to the books you read.

○

Sing songs, play rhyming games, recite nursery rhymes, and chant poems.

○

Help children act out favorite stories.

○

Encourage children to make up silly rhyming words and chants.

Play games that involve giving or following directions, introduce new vocabulary, or involve making sounds.

Provide materials that encourage language development, such as puppets, flannel boards, and any other appropriate material.

Help children write their own books.

**...by encouraging writing**
Have a variety of writing materials available: pencils, markers, paper, blank books, magazines, envelopes, menus, and maps.

Expose children to the power of print aside from books: signs, labels, and so on.

Involve children when you read and write notes that pertain to them.

Find meaningful ways for children to write: labels, signs, notes to family members.

Make sure children see you reading and writing.

Notice and comment on letters and their sounds.

**...with displays**
Display books on shelves that children can reach.

Display classroom books in more than one place, rather than all of them in the book area.

Display letters, words, and other written symbols at children's eye level.

Display children's drawings and writing.

Write down and display children's own language.

Include meaningful print, such as signs and messages, in your learning environment.

**...by supporting language and literacy in the home**
Make families aware of their children's interests, skills, and abilities.

Encourage children to bring favorite books from home to share with the group.

Let children borrow favorite books to take home.

Make sure families know the hours that the public library is open.

Invite family members to be guest readers.

Tell family members about books their child really enjoys.

Schedule bookmaking workshops for families.

Encourage families to provide children with easy access to paper, pencils, markers, and crayons.

# OBSERVING CHILDREN

Observation can be defined as watching and listening in order to learn about individual children. An important ingredient in the learning process is a personal connection between educators and young children. Learning about children through careful observation is the best way to build these all-important personal connections.

Observation personalizes the relationship between educator and child. When you as an educator watch children before taking action, and listen to children before asking questions or making comments, you communicate a very powerful and personal message to children. You are telling children: *I care about you, and I am interested in what you do and say.*

Read the examples that follow. How do you think the educators' observation skills influenced the children's responses? Notice that the educator carefully uses the term *cube* rather than *square* in the first example. It is important to use accurate vocabulary and terms so that children become familiar with this language.

Noah is stringing beads that vary in shape and color. Each time he reaches into the container for another bead, he selects a round one. On two occasions, he pulls out beads that are not round. Both times, he puts them back and picks up round ones. Having observed his process, Mrs. Anderson says, "Noah, why did you put the cube bead back in the bucket?" Noah holds up his string of beads proudly and says, "Because my mother's beads are round like these."

It is outside play time. Jayden and Emma hover over a wet area on the pavement; they have different ideas about what is happening in this wet area. Jayden explains, "No, not the sun! That big dog over there drank the water!" Ms. Redd approaches and says, "It sounds like you have different ideas about what is happening to the puddle. Can you think of a way we could find out about what happens to puddles after it stops raining?" Jayden and Emma are excited. They agree on a plan to put some water in a plate outside the window and watch it to see what happens.

There are situations that involve stepping back from children to watch and listen without interacting with them. For example, you may want to know what activities children are engaged in at a given moment. You might look around your room, noting that a few children are gluing shapes on construction paper, two children are looking at number books, two children are working on an airport puzzle, and another group is building a city with blocks.

This general scan gives you important information about how children are working together in groups. However, it's up to you to take the time to become aware of what's happening with each individual child.

MATH AND SCIENCE INVESTIGATIONS

Consider the individual variations among the children building with blocks in the following examples. What can you learn about each child's understanding of math and science?

> Madison has used four long blocks to make a square on the floor. She is filling it in with smaller blocks in a brick-like pattern. She tells her friends, "I'm making a big parking lot for all the people's cars."

> Daniel has connected a combination of straight and curved blocks end-to-end. He places small cars and trucks on this "road."

> Ava is working on a tall structure. She has stacked blocks that are about 10 inches long in a criss-cross pattern and is counting the layers. She says the building will touch the moon when it's all done.

> Alejandro is using 3" x 3" square blocks and slightly larger pieces of paper to make a row of about 10 small enclosures. They are all the same: four sides and a piece of paper on top. Each little structure has one or more toy people inside. He tells his friends, "This is where a million people live and then I'm gonna make a supermarket so they can get food!"

Because one goal of observation is to establish closer bonds with children and find out about their individual learning styles, pay close attention as they work and talk. What you see and hear will influence how you help them learn. For individual children, you may decide to change some of the following:

○ The kind of questions you ask,
○ The way you answer their questions,
○ The type of assistance you offer,
○ The ideas you share,
○ The information you give, or
○ The materials you provide.

With these thoughts about observation in mind, each investigation in this book includes a section called "Observe Children," which features guiding questions that will help you notice math and science behaviors and language that you can expect to see young children demonstrate.

## DOCUMENTING LEARNING

Documentation plays an important role in children's learning. It is a broad term that simply refers to a record of events. In this book, documentation is referred to in three primary ways—public, professional, and assessment documentation—each having a slightly different purpose:

## PUBLIC DOCUMENTATION

Public documentation is a way to share learning experiences and activities with others, including the children, their families, and other professionals. This type of documentation often takes the form of displays of children's work, actions, and language, accompanied by a written explanation of their educational significance. Public documentation can take many forms:

○ Drawings and paintings with children's transcribed explanations;

○ Displays of sculptures, structures, mobiles, and models with lists of the materials used;

○ Sketches of block structures or designs with children's words about the problems they solved;

○ Photographs of field trips with a written account of the experience; and

○ Graphs showing the results of a survey about "Favorite Food" conducted by children.

## PROFESSIONAL DOCUMENTATION

Professional documentation is intended for an educator's personal use and professional development. It includes strategies educators use to reflect on and plan. There are two tools that will help with this kind of documentation:

○ Reflective journals are records of the experiences and activities that occur in learning situations, as well as the educator's thoughts, questions, opinions, and responses to those events.

○ Webs are graphic organizers that help educators generate ideas for learning experiences that are connected to one another, and therefore, more meaningful to young children.

## ASSESSMENT DOCUMENTATION

*Assessment documentation* is a term used to describe the records educators keep as they observe children's actions and language. These records are used as evidence when educators make overall decisions or judgments about children. Conferences with family members and written reports are much more informative when specific, factual examples are used to support broad, general statements.

There are two main types of assessment documentation:

○ Observational data: brief, written descriptions of children's significant actions, language, and expressions, and

○ Portfolios: collections of children's work (actual samples or photographs) that show performance and progress in key learning areas.

The "Observe Children" sections of each investigation in this book will help you know what to focus on as you gather assessment documentation.

# CONNECTING WITH FAMILIES

Each investigation includes a section called "Connect with Families" that will give you plenty of ideas on how to let families know about the learning experiences their children are having. Here are some other ways to connect with families:

## INFORMATION CONVERSATIONS

In many programs, family members drop off and pick up children. These are perfect opportunities to share an interesting observation or two about individual children. During these conversations, invite families to visit the classroom, ask questions and gather information about their child's interests, and share activities, projects, or special events that involve their child. If you do not see a family member or guardian regularly, you might want to telephone them to share positive news.

## FAMILY CONFERENCES

Scheduling more formal conferences enriches communication with families by allowing time for detailed discussions about learning and creative problem solving. This is an opportunity to show families examples of the investigations that their children enjoy and what their children learned and practiced by doing these investigations. You can refer families to the standards included in this book to show how you have been relating your work with children to math, science, and language and literacy skills and concepts. Display the child's portfolio and other documentation you have assembled to demonstrate the child's progress. Focus on the positive, highlighting the milestones met.

## NEWSLETTERS

Newsletters sent home with children are a great way to share all kinds of information with families. The best ones have a balance of program information and reports about the investigations the children are conducting in the classroom. Here's a list of some ideas for newsletters:

○ List the books you have read and the investigations you have done.
○ Add scanned or photocopied examples of children's work.
○ Put quotes of individual children in the newsletter—be sure to use quotes from all children at some point during the year.
○ Using the language from the "Connect with Families" sections in this book, describe one or two investigations that the children have done and offer a simple way for families to try them at home.
○ Include important program information, such as field trips, upcoming programs, and Family Math and Science nights.
○ Recognize and thank family helpers.

## THE BULLETIN BOARD

A family bulletin board has two important functions. One is to communicate information to families that you want everyone to see, such as "Field Trip Next Week! Bring Boots!" The other function is to promote what is happening in your program. You may want to list the most recent investigation your group has done, using suggestions from the "Connect with Families" sections of this Guide.

## FAMILY INVESTIGATION KITS FOR THE HOME

To extend children's learning into the home, send home an investigation kit in a small bag. This could be something you prepare in advance with a book, materials, and written instructions on how to do the investigation. An investigation kit can be an extension of an investigation that your group has done, or it can be a completely new investigation using the same book.

## FAMILY MATH AND SCIENCE NIGHTS

A Family Math and Science Night is a good way to introduce families to the excitement of what is happening in your program.

Consider presenting an open-ended math or science investigation from this book for families to try. Remember, some families may not have had good experiences with math and science when they were in school. Some may even be a little fearful. This is an opportunity to introduce the skills of math and science to these families and to help them realize, just as the children are learning, that these skills are already part of their daily life and that they can be opportunities to have fun.

# CHAPTER 2

# Measurement, Data Collection, and Graphic Representation

## MEASUREMENT

Young children love to measure: They want to know how tall a skyscraper is, how much something weighs, who is tallest, who is shortest, how far it is to a certain place, or how much time an activity takes.

For young children, measuring begins with the use of nonstandard units of measure that can be any agreed-upon item that represents a unit of measure, such as a chopstick, a hand, an arm-length, or the length of one step away.

Whether it's size, weight, distance, or time, children naturally begin to explore measuring when they ask simple questions such as:

*Is my tower taller than yours?*
*Which tail is longer?*
*Who has more cookies?*

Here are some examples of how you can explore measurement with children every day:

O  Use a variety of nonstandard measuring units to measure, compare, and record your findings.
O  Make good guesses or estimates about measuring.
O  Use rulers, scales, thermometers, measuring cups, and clocks for more exact measurements.
O  Compare measurements and describe things in terms of *longer than*, *shorter than*, *heavier than*, *lighter than*, and *the same as*.

**Some ideas to start you thinking about math:**

**IdeA** When talking about measurements with children, be sure to say the name of the unit. For example, when you ask a child how tall the table is, he or she may say *four*. Respond by saying, *Four what?* If the child has a hard time answering, give a prompt like *We used chopsticks to measure, so the table is four chopsticks tall.*

**Some ideas to start you thinking about science:**

**IdeA** Measurement is an important tool in science. Most science investigations rely on measuring to report outcomes: *How can we find out how much rain fell this month? Which plants have grown tallest? Is my tower taller or shorter than yours?* This data is represented in a variety of ways.

**Some ideas to start you thinking about language and literacy:**

**IdeA** Children love to learn new words—especially big words! Children will enjoy learning and saying the word *measurement* and the words associated with measuring: *comparing, longer than, shorter than, taller than,* and so on.

## VOCABULARY

measure: using a standard to determine the size of an object: My mom uses the kitchen equipment to measure correctly for the cake.

Use books such as these to explore measuring concepts with children:
*Actual Size* by Steve Jenkins
*How Big Is a Foot?* by Rolf Myller
*Twelve Snails to One Lizard* by Susan Hightower
*Just a Little Bit* by Ann Tompert
*Bunny Cakes* by Rosemary Wells

**Note:** Throughout this book there are many opportunities to measure with children.

# INVESTIGATION: MEASURE ME

This investigation uses nonstandard units of measure to help children see how big they really are.

## WHAT'S NEEDED

collection of nonstandard measuring units such as blocks, shoes, chopsticks, or empty soda bottles (You will need enough of each unit so that when laid end to end they are as long as a child.)

masking tape or long strips of paper for a permanent record of heights

> **Read**
>
> Read books such as *How Big Is a Foot?* by Rolf Myller and *Actual Size* by Steve Jenkins while you do this investigation with the children.

## THINGS TO CONSIDER

O How high can the children in your class count? If they cannot count very high, you should use longer measuring units (chopsticks or empty soda bottles). If they like to count very high, use small units (clothespins or paper clips).

O This counting and measuring helps children with math later on when it's time for them to learn to use regular units of measure such as feet and inches.

## KEY MATH STANDARDS CHILDREN PRACTICE

**Communicating:** talking about how many units were used

**Making Connections:** between their own growth and others'

**Numbers and Operations:** counting the units

**Reasoning and Proof:** showing the measurement with concrete objects

## KEY SCIENCE STANDARDS CHILDREN PRACTICE

**Life Science:** talking about relative sizes of children

**Science as Inquiry, Estimating, and Predicting:** using clues to make guesses about size

**Science as Inquiry, Measuring:** making comparisons using nonstandard units of measurement

## STEP BY STEP

1. Ask one child to be a model for this measuring activity. Have the child lie down on the floor. Place a piece of masking tape where the child's head is and the other where his feet are. He can then get up and see how you marked how long he is.

2. Ask the child being measured to choose one of the units for measuring. For example, he might choose blocks.

3. You may want to ask the children to make estimations before measuring. You can say, "How many blocks long do you think Jacob is?" Any estimation is fine; it encourages children to talk about numbers.

4. Help the child place blocks end to end from one piece of tape to the other. In this way, he is measuring how long he is with the blocks. The other children can help him count the total number of blocks. Then say, "Jacob has found out that he is six blocks long."

5. Pairs of children can help each other measure themselves using different objects.

6. You may want to keep a chart of their measurements for discussion and comparison. Later in the year, have the children measure themselves again to see if there are any changes. You can also use long strips of paper to keep a permanent record or make a full-scale graph of children's heights.
   **Note**: It is important (if you want to compare heights) that a "standard" object per child is selected and used. Use the same objects and measure all the children, rather than using different objects to measure different children.

## Talk with Children

○ Listen to the children's comments and questions.

○ Do the children say a number and a unit to describe their measurements? For example, do they say, "I am 10 long," or do they say, "I am 10 straws long?"

○ Do the children use words to compare measurements? *longer than? taller than? shorter than? the same as? equal?*

## Observe Children

○ You might notice that the children are comparing their heights. Katelyn might say that she is taller than Jacob because he is 6 blocks high and she is 8 spoons high. Be prepared to demonstrate that comparisons can be made by using only the same nonstandard unit of measurement. Demonstrate, for example, that a spoon and a block are not the same size.

Notice how the children go about measuring.

○ How do they go about predicting or estimating before actually measuring? Wild guessing? Thinking before guessing?

○ Do the children make a continuous line of nonstandard units that begins and ends on the pieces of tape?

○ Can the children put three or more people in a sequence from shorter to taller?

○ What kinds of questions are the children asking about measuring?

## EXTEND THE LEARNING

○ Some children will be very interested in measuring and counting. Encourage them to measure and compare other things using nonstandard measuring units.

## CONNECT WITH FAMILIES

Display examples of the objects you used for measuring and a chart showing the different lengths of the children along with the following:

Measure Me
_____

We've been using nonstandard units of measure to help us see just how big we really are. When we did this we practiced:

O  Counting,

O  Comparing how tall different people are, and

O  Measuring with objects.

# INVESTIGATION: MAKING PLAYDOUGH

Children explore solids and liquids by measuring and mixing flour, salt, and water as they make their own, nonedible playdough. Children can also experiment with their sense of smell as they add different spices and extracts.

## WHAT'S NEEDED

The following ingredients:

  extracts and spices with different smells: ground cinnamon or anise, vanilla,
    lemon,
  almond, and mint extracts
  4 cups flour
  1 cup salt
  1½ cups water

The following equipment:

  baking tray or cookie sheet
  measuring cups (preferably both liquid and dry)
  mixing bowl and spoon
  something to cover the workspace

_Feast for 10_ by Cathryn Falwell is an excellent book to read with the children while you explore cooking and working together in the kitchen.

## Things to Consider

○ This playdough will not be eaten. This is an investigation to do over and over again. You do not need to do every step each time you present the investigation. Sometimes you will focus on measuring, other times you will focus on describing the physical characteristics of solids and liquids, and other times you will concentrate on describing the different smells.

○ If the children have had limited experience with these ingredients, they'll need some exploration time to experiment, examine, feel, smell, taste, and talk about them. It is okay for children to taste a dab of the different ingredients. Make sure you know about food allergies present in your group and plan accordingly.

○ Prepare a work surface for mixing the dough and for rolling, patting, and forming the dough.

## Key Math Standards Children Practice

Counting cups and spoons while measuring

Making connections and comparisons with other cooking experiences

Measuring: using cups, teaspoons, and tablespoons

## Key Science Standards Children Practice

Physical Science: learning about the different characteristics of solids and liquids, using the sense of touch and smell to describe ingredients

Science as Inquiry: asking questions about what's happening in the investigation

Science as Inquiry: describing changes as the ingredients are mixed and baked

Science as Inquiry: experimenting with various ingredients

Science as Inquiry: making predictions about what will happen to ingredients as they are mixed and baked

## Step by Step

Exploring the Ingredients

Salt: Let the children look at and touch the salt. Ask the children what they notice about the salt:

*What does it look like? What does it feel like? How does it pour? How does it smell? Would you like to taste it?*

Flour: Let the children look at and touch the flour. Ask them what they notice about the flour:

*What does it look like? What does it feel like? How is it the same as the salt? How is it different? How does it smell? Would you like to taste it?*

Water: Let the children look at and touch the water. Ask them what they notice about the water:

*How is it the same as the salt? As the flour? How is it different? How would you describe the water?*

Spices and Extracts: Let the children smell the different spices and extracts. Ask them to describe the different smells, making comparisons to other smells and foods.

## Making Playdough

1. Introduce the children to the measuring cups and spoons.
2. Have the children help pour and measure one cup of salt into a bowl.
3. Measure 1½ cups of warm water in the two-cup measure. Ask:
   *What do you think will happen when I mix the water with the salt?*
4. Add the water to the salt. Encourage the children to take turns stirring the salt-and-water mixture and discuss the changes you see.
5. Help the children use the measuring cups to take turns adding 3½ to 4 cups of flour to the mixture. The children can use their hands to help mix the dough. Mix and knead until the dough is pliable. Talk about textures and how the dough feels after adding the flour. *What changes do you notice?*
6. Divide the dough among the children. Have each child choose a spice or extract and help all the children knead a very small amount of scent into their dough.
7. The children can roll and shape the dough with their hands or use plastic knives or cookie cutters to cut out shapes.
8. When the children are ready to bake their shapes, place them on a baking tray. Ask the children to predict what will happen when the objects are baked. *How do you think your dough will change?*
9. Bake in an oven at 250°F until the dough is hard. Baking time will vary with the size and thickness of the shapes. After the tray of playdough comes out of the oven and has cooled down, talk with the children about their predictions.

## Talk with Children

○ Allow the children time to examine the measuring cups before using them.
   *What do you notice about these cups?*
   *How are they different from other kinds of cups?*
   *Where else have you used cups like these?*
○ Point out the lines on the liquid cup measures.
○ Count aloud as you add ingredients and divide and distribute the dough.
○ Encourage the children to use descriptive words to describe how the playdough feels and smells, such as *soft, powdery, dry, wet, sticky, pungent, strong, sweet,* and *fruity.*
○ As often as possible, use math and science vocabulary such as *dissolve, solid, liquid, quarter, half,* and *full.* Use shape vocabulary whenever possible. Use comparative words such as *smaller, larger, more than, less than,* and *the same as.*
○ Encourage the children to make predictions about what changes they will see when the water is added to the flour and when the dough is baked.

### Observe Children

○ How do the children use the measuring cups? (understand what "full" means? pay attention to the lines? ignore the lines?)

○ How do the children describe the ingredients? (by naming them? comparing them to other substances? using descriptive words?)

○ What are the different ways the children are involved in this investigation? (as an observer? by being hesitant and very neat? by being fully involved with flour all over themselves? by being silent? noisy?)

○ What kinds of questions do children ask? (*What's that? Why? What would happen if...?*)

### EXTEND THE LEARNING

○ There are many different recipes for playdough. Try several and keep track of the children's descriptions of how they are the same and different.

○ Try some edible cooking projects (cookies, pancakes, muffins) that use similar ingredients.

○ Allow the children many opportunities to measure and mix!

### CONNECT WITH FAMILIES

Display the playdough recipe and the children's playdough, along with the following:

## Making Playdough

We made playdough out of salt and flour dough. When we made playdough we practiced:

○ Using measuring cups and spoons;

○ Exploring solids and liquids;

○ Noticing how things can be changed by mixing and cooking;

○ Using new words like *solid, liquid, dissolve* and *absorb, strong, fruity* and *pungent*; and

○ Counting.

# DATA COLLECTION AND GRAPHIC REPRESENTATION

Collecting data and representing that data are key mathematics skills. Charts and other graphic representations are useful tools that help young children organize, analyze, and understand information in a visual form. For young children, graphic representation can be simple drawings. Data can be collected in a variety of ways, and these representations help children answer questions, visualize data, and make comparisons and predictions. Some examples follow:

**T-Charts** help us analyze same and different between two objects or events.

**Bar Graphs** help us compare things. We easily see the relationships of *less than*, *more than*, and *same as*.

**Block Bar Graphs** are three-dimensional bar graphs made from building blocks or linking cubes that are arranged on paper, representing the number of objects or events being graphed.

**Pictographs** are similar to bar graphs but use pictures instead of blocks or linking cubes to represent the objects or events being graphed.

**Pie or Circle Graphs** show how the whole collection of data is divided into parts or fractions having specific attributes.

**Sorting Loops** are lengths of shoelaces, yarn, or string that are shaped into circles, which are used for grouping sets of items.

**Tally Charts** provide spaces for counting and recording objects or events. Each mark on a tally sheet represents one object or event.

**Concept Maps** are diagrams that show the relationships among themes and ideas.

Many measuring devices display information in a graphic manner: thermometers, calendars, schedules, clocks, and auto dashboard displays are all visual representations of data being collected in a different way and place.

Examples of graphic representation follow on the next two pages and throughout the manual.

Informal comparing, classifying, and counting activities can provide the mathematical beginnings for developing young learners' understanding of data, analysis of data, and statistics. Children do this as they:

O  Pose questions and gather data about themselves and their surroundings.

O  Sort and classify objects according to their attributes and organize data about the objects.

O  Represent data using concrete objects, pictures and graphs.

—NCTM 2000, p. 108

# EXAMPLES OF GRAPHIC REPRESENTATION

Birthday Pictograph

| | |
|---|---|
| Jan | 🚶 |
| Feb | |
| Mar | 🚶 |
| Apr | |
| May | 🚶 🚶 🚶 |
| June | |
| July | 🚶 🚶 🚶 🚶 |
| Aug | |
| Sept | 🚶 🚶 |
| Oct | 🚶 🚶 🚶 |
| Nov | |
| Dec | 🚶 |

## WHEN ARE OUR BIRTHDAYS?

The children participate in making a pictograph, placing a figure in the column next to the month in which they were born. Suggested questions:

*What do you notice about our pictograph?*

*Which month has the most birthdays?*

*Which has the least? How do you know?*

*Is there a month when no one has a birthday?*

*Are there months with the same number of birthdays?*

Let's count and write the numbers, telling us "How many?" for each month.

## WHAT'S OUR FAVORITE…?

The children discover the group's favorite and least favorite pizza topping (or anything else) by asking a question and making a block bar graph. Suggested questions:

*What do you notice about our graph?*

*What is our favorite pizza topping?*

*Which is the least favorite?*

*How do we know?*

Let's count and write the numbers, telling us "How many?" for each topping.

Pepperoni

Vegetable

Plain

Other

## HOW MANY…?

The children collect data and see how many times it rained on their story time day. Ask:

*What do you notice about our T-chart?*

*Did we have more days with rain or without rain? How do we know?*

April Story Time Days

rain ☔ | not rain ☀️☁️

## WHERE WERE WE BORN?

The children make a "live" pie graph to see who was born in their home state, who was born in other states, and who was born in other countries.

To make the graph: Sort the group. Everyone born in Our (your home state) State makes a set (group), everyone born in Other States makes a group, and everyone born in Other Countries makes a group.

Everyone joins hands to make a circle with each of the sorted groups standing together (see illustration).

A piece of colored yarn is placed around the entire group so that each group is standing together on the edge of the circle.

Make the graph by placing yarn from the center of the circle to the edge of the circle, dividing the groups (see illustration above). Ask questions such as the following:

*What do you notice about our graph?*
*Where were most of us born? How do you know?*
*What else can we tell from looking at our graph?*

Measurement...

# CHAPTER 3

# More than Counting

Most people who work with young children do fingerplays every day. Usually it's counting down as in "Five Little Ducks"—One flew away and then there were four. You always pause before saying the number and all the children say: "Four!"

For young children, number sense is about understanding the different uses for numbers. Number sense is the ability to count, to be able to continue counting—or count on—from a specific number as well as to count backwards, to count an object only once, to see relationships between numbers, to be able to take a specific number apart and put it back together again. It is about making sets, adding, and subtracting.

Today you decide to use five large objects to extend this counting. Sitting on the floor together, you place five puppets in front of the children. Several children take turns counting the puppets. You notice that some children touch the puppets as they count, some just say the numbers aloud. You ask one boy who hasn't participated if he would like to count the puppets and indeed he touches the puppets and counts to five.

You realize that even though several of the children are not yet four, everyone in the group understands one-to-one correspondence. You can build on this mathematical knowledge with stories and activities in future programs.

Research has shown that young children are sophisticated mathematical thinkers. Children as young as age two develop oral counting skills and use number words. They acquire many more math skills and concepts before they enter kindergarten. Acquiring these skills and concepts provides an important base for future math learning.

Circle or group times and other daily routines provide opportunities for exploring numbers and operations, while developing children's math skills, concepts, and vocabulary.

Reading picture books and doing hands-on activities strengthen the development of children's math concepts and skills as you ask open-ended questions, encourage children to explain what they're doing, and provide many experiences with the same number or operation, such as doing many different activities using one number or making and counting sets with a variety of manipulative materials.

Even the youngest children love to talk about and explore numbers:
- José says, "Look, Ms. Wilson! I see numbers everywhere! On the clock, on Emmett's sock, even on that chart and on the door!"
- Jasmine holds up four fingers and says, "I'm four years old!"
- Henry and Sarah share the plate of cookies: "One for you, one for me…"

Begin your number activities working up to and including only those numbers that children understand.

It's easy to assess children's number knowledge. Hold up three fingers and ask your group:
*How many fingers am I holding up?*
*Can you each show me three fingers?*

Randomly ask children to count aloud the fingers they're holding up. Repeat this with four fingers, then five fingers, and so on.

## Some ideas to start you thinking about math:

**Idea** In the past, learning mathematics focused on memorizing number facts, shape names, how many inches in a foot, algebraic formulas, and so on. Today, the emphasis in mathematics is on using mathematical information to think through a variety of problems.

**Some ideas to start you thinking about science:**

**Idea** Understanding numbers and operations is important for all science investigations. When children collect data, ask questions, and represent what they observe and learn, they must have an understanding of mathematics skills and concepts.

**Some ideas to start you thinking about language and literacy:**

**Idea** Almost any picture book provides opportunities to explore numbers and operations. In counting books, look for clear representations of one-to-one correspondence and other math concepts. Introduce new vocabulary such as *numeral* and *set*, and help children understand terms such as *more than*, *less than*, and *equal to*.

## VOCABULARY

**addition:** the process of calculating the sum of two or more numbers or amounts

**equal:** identical in size or quantity

**equal sign:** a mathematical symbol (=) used to indicate that two or more numbers have the same value as each other

**number:** quantity represented by a word or symbol

**numeral:** the written symbol referring to a number

**one-to-one correspondence:** verbal-object counting skill (counting an object only once)

**operations:** a mathematical function or action such as addition or subtraction

**part-part-whole:** recognizing part-part-whole relationships (taking numbers apart and putting them back together) is a basic in developing number sense

**set:** a group or collection of objects

**subtraction:** the process of deducting one number or quantity from another

When you use counting books with children, make sure they feature clear one-to-one correspondence. Here are a few suggestions:

*Anno's Counting Book* by Mitsumasa Anno
*Ten, Nine, Eight* by Molly Bang
*How Do You Count a Dozen Ducklings?* by In Seon Chae
*My Numbers / Mis Numeros* by Rebecca Emberley
*1, 2, Buckle My Shoe* by Anna Grossnickle Hines
*Feast for 10* by Cathryn Falwell
*10 Minutes Till Bedtime* by Peggy Rathmann
*Seven Blind Mice* by Ed Young

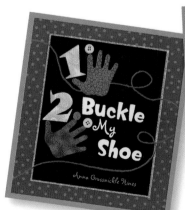

# INVESTIGATION: I KNOW 3, THREE, ▲▲▲

Children count and represent numbers, beginning with the number 3.

## WHAT'S NEEDED
counters (small objects)
small paper plates
strips of colored paper
yarn or string (for making loops)

Read a book like *Seven Blind Mice* by Ed Young with the children while you do this investigation.

## THINGS TO CONSIDER
○ What do the children already know about numbers? Adapt this investigation as needed.

## KEY MATH STANDARDS CHILDREN PRACTICE
**Numbers and Operations:** count an object only once, using one-to-one correspondence
**Numbers and Operations:** count and learn the sequence of numbers
**Numbers and Operations:** count with understanding and recognize "how many" in a set of objects
**Numbers and Operations:** recognize and name written numerals, develop a sense of quantity: know that the word "three" and the symbol "3" mean a quantity of something

## STEP BY STEP
1. Talk with the children about the number 3. Can children think of any nursery rhymes or stories that feature three characters? (Hint: *The Three Little Kittens, The Three Little Pigs, Goldilocks and the Three Bears*. Mention the other words that designate 3: *trio, triplet,* and so on.)
2. Allow the children plenty of time to explore your materials. How many different ways can they make 3? Try the following:
   *Making different groups (sets) of 3 objects. Place each group in a loop.*
   *What other ways can you make 3?*
3. Write the numeral *3* and the word *three* on two paper plates.
4. Take turns counting the objects in each group of objects and matching either the word or the numeral to that set.
5. When children are ready to count higher, choose another number and repeat the activity.

MATH AND SCIENCE INVESTIGATIONS

### Talk with Children

○ When the children count, remind them to count each object only once. Take time to practice counting with each child as often as possible.

○ Listen to what the children say as they make their sets.

### Observe Children

○ Which children touch the objects as they count them? Which children count aloud? Which children can recognize a set of three without counting them?

## EXTEND THE LEARNING: BUILD A NUMBER CREATURE!

Combine number awareness and creativity to make creatures.

## WHAT'S NEEDED

art materials such as stickers, feathers, toothpicks, craft sticks, chenille sticks, and yarn
cut-out paper shapes
glue or glue sticks
number die
paper towel tubes
scissors
tape

## STEP BY STEP

1. The children roll the die and choose materials based on the number rolled on the die. Use a paper tube for the base. The tubes can be used horizontally or vertically to make a "creature."

2. Each child creates a creature by attaching the correct number of materials to the tube-base. For example, if the child rolled a 4, he or she might attach four feathers, four wings, four strips of paper for stripes, four stickers for eyes, and so on.

3. Make a label for the creature that includes the number. Have the children take turns rolling the die and building a creature to take home.

(Adapted from NCTM's *Showcasing Mathematics for the Young Child*, 2004.)

## CONNECT WITH FAMILIES

Display the children's work with the following information:

We've been making three—and more! When we did this, we:

O Counted objects,

O Practiced one-to-one correspondence,

O Recognized and named written numerals,

O Made our own Number Creatures, and

O Had fun!

Concepts that form the core of young children's number sense and understanding:

Use numbers to quantify sets (collections):

*How many fingers do you have on one hand?*

Use numbers to compare sets:

*I have three books and Connor has two books.*

Add and subtract single-digit numbers:

*I have three blocks. If I give you one block, I will have two for myself.*

Understand part-part-whole relationships:

*If we have six children and four of them sit at one table and two sit at another table, do we still have six children?*

Understand equal partitioning or grouping:

*There are four cookies. It's fair if we each have two cookies.*

MATH AND SCIENCE INVESTIGATIONS

# INVESTIGATION: MAKE YOUR OWN COUNTING BOOK

Children design and make a number-and-counting book.

## WHAT'S NEEDED

blank book for each child

catalogs for cutting out pictures

crayons

markers

materials such as stickers and other materials

scissors

stamps and stamp pads or stampers

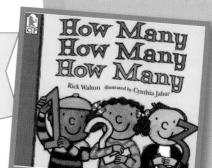

Read counting books, such as *1, 2, Buckle My Shoe* by Anna Grossnickle Hines and *How Many How Many How Many* by Rick Walton, with the children while you do this investigation.

## THINGS TO CONSIDER

○ Read through this investigation and think about the developmental level of your group. Can you do this with the whole group or is it better to work with small groups?

○ Making counting books can be very simple or quite complicated. You will know best how many pages to give children. Depending on your situation, the books can be worked on over several days.

## KEY MATH STANDARDS CHILDREN PRACTICE

**Communicating:** sharing the counting books and telling others about what comes next

**Geometry and Spatial Sense:** naming and describing basic shapes in the counting books and using words that describe where objects are located within each book

**Making Connections:** talking about familiar counting books

**Numbers and Operations:** counting and making counting books as well as having a sense of quantity

## STEP BY STEP

1. Talk together about how a counting book can be made. You might ask:

   *If we start with the number one in our counting book, what comes next?*

   *What comes after two?*

   *How can we represent one? Two? Three?*

2. Tell the children that they can make their own counting books. Brainstorm a list of "counting book ideas" with the children. Some ideas include cars, cookies,

children, trees, houses, or flowers, or something simpler to draw, such as balls, circles, or dots.

Explain to your group that the counting books can be illustrated in a variety of ways: with magazine or catalog pictures, stampers, stickers, crayons—whatever materials you have.

Some children may make a counting book counting to ten while others may not count past five.

3. When all books are completed, help children share their counting books with the whole group.

## Talk with Children

O As the children work on their books, ask questions such as the following:
*What number comes next?*
*How many shapes will you draw/put with that number?*

O Encourage the children to represent numbers in as many ways as possible: 1, one, first, solo, single.

## Observe Children

O As the children draw and count, you'll notice important math behaviors.

O Some children may know what number comes next without counting from one. Others may need to count from one each time.

O Which children use their fingers to count as they say each number and which children have some difficulty with this? Who needs help writing numbers?

O Are the children saying the numbers in the correct order?

O How high can different children count?

O What do the children say when you ask how many are on a certain page? Do they say the total number or do they count each object?

MATH AND SCIENCE INVESTIGATIONS

# EXTEND THE LEARNING: PAPER NUMBER CHAINS

Count and represent numbers using counters and by making paper chains.

## WHAT'S NEEDED

counters
glue or glue sticks
paper strips in a variety of colors

## STEP BY STEP

1. Divide the children into small groups. Each group will need counters, paper strips, glue or glue sticks, and an adult to help.
2. Show the children how to make a paper chain. Have the children select the number of counters they'd like to represent with their paper chains.
3. When the chains are completed, have the children explain what they created by counting the number of links.

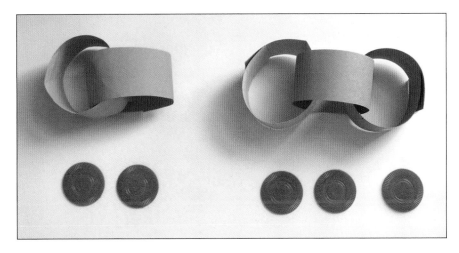

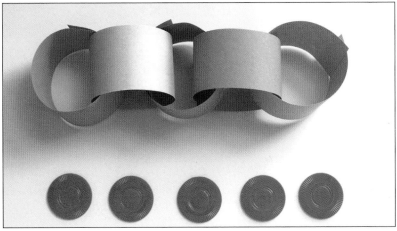

## CONNECT WITH FAMILIES

Display your group's counting books and the following information:

### Make Your Own Counting Book

We made counting books! While we made our books we practiced:

O Counting and using numbers to explain quantity,

O Naming numbers, and

O Making books and telling each other which number comes next.

# INVESTIGATION: DOMINOES

As children play with dominoes they count and compare the dots, examine the dot patterns, and learn to play a dominoes game.

## WHAT'S NEEDED

index cards or paper plates with numerals written on them
one or two sets of dominoes

Read a book such as *Hannah's Collections* by Marthe Jocelyn while you do this investigation.

## THINGS TO CONSIDER

○ Allow the children plenty of time to freely explore dominoes before using them in a structured way.

○ You will probably discover that in one group of children there are many different levels of number awareness and counting skills. Observe carefully and try to help the children at their own levels.

## KEY MATH STANDARDS CHILDREN PRACTICE

**Communicating:** using math language, describing the arrangement of dots, using number words

**Numbers and Operations:** counting, developing a sense of quantity, and doing beginning addition

**Patterns, Functions, and Algebra:** recognizing dot patterns and connecting them to certain quantities

## STEP BY STEP

1. Put the dominoes out on a table and let the children experiment with them. When the children first play with the dominoes, observe what they do. Do they invent their own games? Do they count the dots? Do they use the dominoes to build?

2. Help the children notice that when there is one pip (or dot), it is always in the middle, two pips are always in opposite corners, three pips are in a diagonal row. Learning to see that each number has its own pattern of pips will help the children recognize the number of pips more quickly.

3. Place the collection of dominoes in a bag or box. Have each child choose a domino and count the pips. Have the children compare the number of pips with a partner. Which domino has more?

4. Ask the children to form groups based on the number of pips on their dominoes. Everyone with three pips would get together, and so on. Give each group their corresponding numeral card. Which number was the most common?

5. Remix the dominoes and repeat, using larger numbers. Have the children make a drawing of their pip groups to take home.

### Talk with Children

○ Model counting the dots by pointing to each dot as you say the numbers.

○ Ask the children:

*What do you notice about the dots on the dominoes?*

○ Encourage the children to notice that the patterns of dots are consistent:

*Look, four dots are always in a square!*

○ Use math vocabulary:

*The three dots are in a diagonal line.*

○ Help the children count the dots if they have a hard time matching equal numbers of dots. Talk about how when you count, you count each dot only once. Recognize when children are not developmentally ready to count the larger groups of dots.

### Observe Children

○ What kinds of things do the children do when they're playing with the dominoes? (make designs? make "roads"? make towers? stand them on end in a row and tip over the first one to see the rest fall? sort them in different ways? invent games?)

○ How do children count the dots on the dominoes? (by pointing? just by looking? by guessing? other ways?)

○ How do children match dominoes? (by counting both sets of dots? by putting them side by side to see if they look the same? other ways?)

○ How do children describe the patterns of dots? (with vague descriptions—One there and one there? by comparing the pattern to something—It looks like footprints? by using shape names—Four dots make a square?)

## EXTEND THE LEARNING: PLAY A DOMINOES GAME!

### WHAT'S NEEDED

set of dominoes

two or more players (The more players you have, the more domino sets you will need.)

### STEP BY STEP

1. Place all the dominoes face down on the table and mix them up.
2. Each player takes seven dominoes and stands them up with the pips facing the player so that the players can't see each other's dominoes. The remaining dominoes become the "draw" pile.
3. The first player places a domino (from his seven dominoes) in the center of the table.
4. The second player then tries to match one of her dominoes to either end or the side (if the domino is a doubles) of the domino in play. Only one domino is played at each turn. If a player cannot match the pips at any open row, she must pick from the draw pile until she is able to play a domino.

5. The game continues until one player has used up all his dominoes. If no one can play a domino, the player with no dominoes or the least number of points (pips) wins the round.

**Note**: Young children can learn to play with their dominoes faceup (pips showing).

## CONNECT WITH FAMILIES

Display photographs of children using dominoes, pictures of dominoes that show the different ways to arrange them, and examples of the observations children made about dominoes, along with the following:

Dominoes

We investigated a set of dominoes. When we looked at dominoes and examined the patterns evident in the arrangement of dots, we practiced:

O  One-to-one correspondence and counting skills,

O  Looking for patterns in numbers, and

O  Playing a dominoes game.

# INVESTIGATION: COUNT AND MATCH SETS

Children make sets, count "how many," and create matching number sets.

## WHAT'S NEEDED

crayons or markers

index cards or paper plates with numerals written on them

objects for counting such as dominoes, counters, linking cubes, and buttons

paper

Read a book such as *12 Ways to Get to 11* by Eve Merriam while you do this investigation with the children.

## THINGS TO CONSIDER

O  Be sure children are familiar with lower numbers before progressing to larger numbers.

## KEY MATH STANDARDS CHILDREN PRACTICE

**Numbers and Operations:** count an object only once, using one-to-one correspondence

**Numbers and Operations:** count and learn the sequence of numbers

**Numbers and Operations:** count with understanding and recognize "how many" in a set of objects

**Numbers and Operations:** recognize and name written numerals, use comparative terms such as *more than*, *less than*, and *equal to*

## STEP BY STEP

1. Allow the children time to explore, talk about, and count the various objects.
2. Show the children how the objects can be counted and arranged in a set (group, collection). Make and count sets of three, four, and more. As you make a set, ask: *Can you make a set using different objects to match my set?*
3. Help the children decide which number they want to represent. Challenge them to make matching sets of that number with as many materials as possible. Talk about the sets children have made. Ask them to count and describe their sets.
4. Have the children make a drawing of one or more of their sets. An adult helper can write the numeral on the drawing.
5. Repeat this activity many times, using higher numbers as children learn to count accurately using one-to-one correspondence.

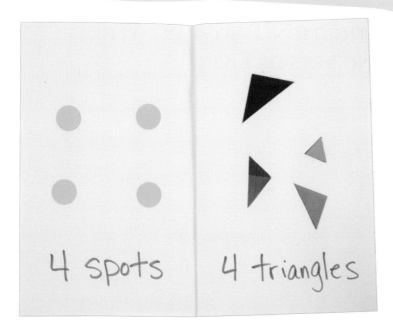

4 spots | 4 triangles

## Talk with Children

○ When the children count, remind them to count each object only once. Take time to practice counting with each child as often as possible.

○ Listen to what the children say as they make their sets.

## Observe Children

○ What do the children do to make their sets?

○ What strategies do the children use to make their sets? Do some children count each object in each set?

○ Can the children count one group of objects, and then count another, without starting at one again? For instance, if they have three chips in one group and four in another, do they count "1, 2, 3" and then "1, 2, 3, 4"? Or do they count "1, 2, 3, 4, 5, 6, 7"?

○ With younger children, you may want to start with just three objects. Challenge the children to make as many sets as possible.

## EXTEND THE LEARNING

○ Make a set of numeral cards and do this investigation again. Challenge the children to find the numeral card to match each set they make.

## CONNECT WITH FAMILIES

### Count and Match Sets

We have been counting and making sets. When we did this investigation we practiced:

○ Display examples of children's sets. Post the following on your bulletin board:

○ Counting each object only once—this is called one-to-one correspondence, and

○ Counting with understanding and recognizing "how many" in a set of objects.

# INVESTIGATION: PART-PART-WHOLE: MAKING SETS OF FIVE

Children learn more about sets and addition as you take apart numbers and put them back together.

## WHAT'S NEEDED

crayons
paper
pompoms (soft objects)
**Note**: Soft objects work best because they won't roll so far away when dropped from a distance above.
string or yarn to create circles

Read a book such as *How Do You Count a Dozen Ducklings?* by In Seon Chae while you do this investigation with the children.

## THINGS TO CONSIDER

O This is an active investigation. Children will need clear instructions and supervision.

## KEY MATH STANDARDS CHILDREN PRACTICE

**Numbers and Operations:** begin to understand addition by counting groups of objects, use comparative terms such as *more than, less than* and *the same as* or *equal to*

**Numbers and Operations:** count and learn the sequence of numbers

**Numbers and Operations:** count with understanding and recognize "how many" in a set of objects

**Numbers and Operations:** develop a sense of whole numbers by composing and decomposing numbers

**Numbers and Operations:** learn to count an object only once, using one-to-one correspondence

## STEP BY STEP

1. Make two string or yarn circles on the floor, large enough for several children to gather around.
2. Give each child five pompoms and have the children take turns dropping the pompoms one by one into the circle. After one child drops the pompoms, ask:
   *How many are inside the circle?*
   *How many are outside the circle?*
   *Do you still have five pompoms? Let's count them: "Three on the outside plus two on the inside equals…?*
3. Try this several times, asking the same questions. Talk about *more than* and *less than*, and *equal to*.

MATH AND SCIENCE INVESTIGATIONS

4. Make drawings of your inside and outside sets.
5. Try this with eight or 10 pompoms.

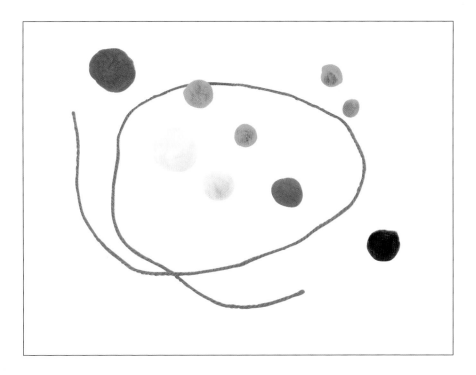

## Talk with Children

○ Talk with the children about *more than*, *less than*, and *equal to*. Take time to practice counting with each child. Listen to what the children say when they drop their pompoms. Do they talk about "adding" one more pompom to the circle?

## Observe Children

○ Which children can count without touching each pompom? Which children need to touch them to keep track?

○ Which children understand "three on the outside plus two on the inside equals five"? Can the children count one set of pompoms and then count another without starting at one again? For example, if they have three pompoms inside and two inside, do they count "1, 2, 3…" and then "1, 2" or do they count "1, 2, 3, 4, 5"?

## EXTEND THE LEARNING: SETS OF SEVEN

Continue number investigations from sets of five to sets of seven.

## WHAT'S NEEDED

objects such as linking cubes, counter, or other common objects

## STEP BY STEP

1. Challenge the children to make sets of seven with the objects. Give each child seven counters. Ask the children to carefully count the cubes (or the objects they are using) to be sure they each have seven.

2. Ask the children to divide the counters into a set of six and a set of one.
   *How many sets do you have?*
   *How many counters are in each set?*
   *Do you still have seven counters?*

3. Have the children remix the counters into one set of seven. Work together to make sets using the seven counters. How many different ways can you make seven?

4. Talk about and represent the ways the children have made sets with their counters. Help the children make and label a drawing of some of their sets.

## CONNECT WITH FAMILIES

### Part-Part-Whole: Making Sets Five

○ Display children's sets and post the following:

We've been practicing how many ways you can make five and then how many ways you can make seven. We're beginning to understand addition by counting groups of objects. In this investigation, we learned to:

○ Count with understanding,

○ Understand how many in a set of objects, and

○ Use comparative terms such as *more than*, *less than*, and *equal to*.

# CHAPTER 4
# Out and About

The outside world is a very exciting place for young children. It is easy to understand why most children love outdoor adventures. The sounds, sights, smells, and textures appeal to children's sense of wonder and curiosity.

The outside world is loaded with opportunities for children to develop important math and science understandings and skills. As they walk through puddles, go up and down hills, maneuver around obstacles, watch the sky, and examine the ground, children gather information and practice investigation skills.

When they are outside, children are able to:
- Use all of their senses;
- Notice organized patterns;
- See similarities and differences;
- Make predictions;
- Notice changes;
- Learn to care for and respect the environment, creatures, and plants;
- Describe where things are;
- Move in different directions; and
- Identify the shapes of objects.

Watch and listen to children as they discuss their outside activities. You may witness extraordinary learning taking place. Consider these examples:

> Sarah and Jamal are collecting leaves. As they gather the leaves together, they notice that some leaves are small and shaped like circles, while others are large and pointy. Sarah says, "Look! This leaf is turning red. That means fall is coming."

> Joshua asked Daniel how to get to his house. Daniel says, "First you go past the fire house and at the stop sign, turn to the white house. Count three more houses and my house is by the big tree."

**Some ideas to start you thinking about math:**

**Idea**    Charts and other graphic representations are useful tools that help young children organize, analyze, and understand information in a visual form. For young children, graphic representation can be simple drawings. Data can be collected in a variety of ways and these representations help children answer questions, visualize data, and make comparisons and predictions.

**Some ideas to start you thinking about science:**

**Idea**    For young children, going places is like experimenting in a science laboratory. They gather information and ask questions; they find organized patterns and make comparisons; they make estimates and predictions. As they do these things, they talk—naming, describing, hypothesizing, and explaining. The world is a laboratory for all branches of science—physical science, life science, earth and space science, and design technology.

**Some ideas to start you thinking about language and literacy:**

**Idea**    Picture books—both fiction and nonfiction—offer opportunities for children to learn about, talk about, and experience the world around them. Because the vocabulary in books is more complex and diverse than everyday conversation, children learn new words and ways of expressing ideas. In addition, they see representations (pictures) of the words being used.

## VOCABULARY

**atmosphere:** the mixture of gases that surround a celestial body such as the Earth

**climate:** the average of weather over time and space

**light:** the energy producing a sensation of brightness that makes seeing possible

**season:** one of the major divisions of the year generally based on yearly period changes in weather

**shadow:** a darkened shape on a surface that falls behind somebody or something blocking the light

Here are a few book suggestions for shadows and weather exploration:

*Moonbear's Shadow* by Frank Asch

*What Makes a Shadow?* by Clyde Robert Bulla

*Down Comes the Rain* by Franklyn Branley

*One Hot Summer Day* by Nina Crews

*Weather Words and What They Mean* by Gail Gibbons

*Come on, Rain!* by Karen Hesse

*The Snowy Day* by Ezra Jack Keats

# INVESTIGATION: OUTSIDE SHADOWS

In this investigation, children create different shadows with their bodies and with other objects.

## WHAT'S NEEDED

several objects, such as an umbrella, a broom, a hoop, or a jump rope

sidewalk chalk or tape for marking or tracing shadows

space where it will be easy to see and play with shadows

sunny day

> A book such as *Moonbear's Shadow* by Frank Asch is an excellent introduction to shadow exploration.

## THINGS TO CONSIDER

O The children will be very active in this investigation.

## KEY MATH STANDARDS CHILDREN PRACTICE

**Geometry and Spatial Sense:** describing where shadows are in relation to each other

**Measuring:** comparing and measuring the length of shadows

## KEY SCIENCE STANDARDS CHILDREN PRACTICE

**Earth and Space Science:** investigating the shape, position, and change in shadows
**Science as Inquiry:** noticing change over time as shadows change
**Science as Inquiry:** observing and gathering information about shadows
**Science as Inquiry:** predicting and checking what happens

## STEP BY STEP

1. On the first day of shadow play, encourage the children to have fun with their shadows. Some things the children might try:
   Make their shadows touch another person's shadow without touching the other person.
   Make shadows with four arms.
   Try to hide their shadows.

   You and your group will have other ideas to try once you begin playing with shadows.

2. On another sunny day, experiment with different objects outside that will make interesting shadows. Encourage the children to make as many different shadows as they can with their bodies and the objects.

### Talk with Children

- Challenge the children to find out how shadows change over time on a sunny day.
- Look at and talk about the shadows of things outside such as a fence, swing set, or a bicycle. Do these shadows change over time on a sunny day? How can you find out?

### Observe Children

- Notice how the children go about exploring and investigating shadows. Some children will invent many different ways to make their shadows do different things. Other children will get their ideas from watching their friends.
  - Which children sustain and extend their interest in shadow play?
    - Listen to the children talk about shadows. What words do the children use to describe the shadows they create?
      - What questions are they asking about shadows? How do the children respond to your questions about shadows?

MATH AND SCIENCE INVESTIGATIONS

## EXTEND THE LEARNING: FOLLOW THAT SHADOW!

### WHAT'S NEEDED
a sunny place
stone
stick, chalk, or tape

### STEP BY STEP
1. Find a sunny place in the grass or dirt.
2. Use a stick, chalk, or tape to mark where a child's toes are so that later he or she can stand in the exact same place.
3. On the shadow of the child's head, place a stone or mark the place with tape or chalk.
4. Leave the spot and come back a half hour later (or longer) and do step three again with the child's feet in the original position.
5. Repeat several times. What pattern do the stones or tape make after several hours?

### CONNECT WITH FAMILIES
○ Display photographs of this investigation.
○ Post the following on your bulletin board:

### Outside Shadows
We went outside to explore shadows. While we were outside, we experimented with our shadows, making them large and small, hiding them, and playing Shadow Tag. We also learned about the relationship between the sun and shadows. When we did this investigation we practiced:
- Measuring and comparing lengths, and
- Using spatial and positional words as we described where shadows were in relation to each other.

# INVESTIGATION: INSIDE SHADOWS

Children explore how light can create shadows of different sizes and shapes.

## WHAT'S NEEDED

flashlight

paper

small objects such as plastic animals, cars, or people

tape

**Note**: If you have several flashlights, the children will be able to extend their explorations.

Read a book such as *Moonbear's Shadow* by Frank Asch to further explore shadows with the children.

## THINGS TO CONSIDER

O  What do children already know about shadows? Before doing this activity talk together about shadows and how they are made. If you've already done the Outdoor Shadows investigation, remind children about the relationship between the sun (as the light source) and shadows.

## KEY SCIENCE STANDARDS CHILDREN PRACTICE

**Physical Science:** learning about light, shadows, and opaque objects

**Science as Inquiry:** estimating and predicting how long shadows will be and what shapes they will have

**Science as Inquiry:** experimenting with different objects to make shapes

**Science as Inquiry:** recognizing the relationship between an object and its shadows

## STEP BY STEP

1. Cover a table with white paper. Move the table so that it is against a wall and put white paper on the wall, too. At the other end of the table, tape a flashlight to the table so that the flashlight cannot be moved.

2. Place small objects on the table and turn on the flashlight. You will see the shadows on the table and on the wall.

3. Allow the children plenty of time to experiment with the objects and making shadows. Engage the group in a conversation about what you notice.

4. Unfasten the flashlight. Allow the children time to move the light over and around the objects. Challenge the children to make the shadows bigger or smaller. Can they make the shadows dance? Can anyone make it look like one animal is eating another animal?

## Talk with Children

○ Questions you can ask the children as they investigate making shadows include:

*Can you make a long shadow?*

*Can you make a short shadow?*

*Is the shadow always the same shape as the object?*

*Can you make a shadow that fools us so we cannot guess what the object is?*

## Observe Children

○ Notice the similarities and differences between what the children do in this investigation and what they did in "Outside Shadows."

○ How do the children use their experiences from the "Outside Shadows" investigation in this one? Do they try to imitate their movements in that activity by using the small objects?

○ Do the children seem intentional as they experiment with the small shadows, or is their play experimental or random in nature? What are your clues?

○ Are the children interested in telling a story with the figures and light? Are they comfortable enough with shadows and light to make up their own dramatic play?

○ Listen to the children's language to understand their thinking. Do they make comparisons among different kinds of shadows? What do they actually say?

## EXTEND THE LEARNING

○ Continue learning about light and shadow by placing one object on a piece of paper on a table. Use the flashlight and pretend it's the sun. Use it to make a shadow of the object on the paper.

○ Keep the flashlights and objects available for further shadow investigation.

## CONNECT WITH FAMILIES

○ Display the flashlight and some of the objects used in the investigation. Suggest that the families use the flashlight and objects to make as many different shadows as they can.

○ Post the following on the bulletin board:

### Inside Shadows

We've been using flashlights and plastic objects to experiment with shadows. We learned about light and shadows. When we did this investigation, we practiced:

▪ Estimating and predicting how long shadows will be, and

▪ Making shapes from different objects.

# INVESTIGATION: BE FRIENDS WITH A TREE

Children use science and math to look at a tree and its surroundings and to notice changes over time.

## WHAT'S NEEDED

camera
clipboards (if you have them)
first-aid kit
magnifying glasses
markers or crayons
paper
tree that you can regularly visit with your group to observe a yearly cycle
**Note**: You'll need time to visit the tree at least once a month over the course of several seasons.

Read books about plant growth such as *Jody's Beans* by Malachy Doyle while you do this investigation with the children.

## THINGS TO CONSIDER

O You will want to collect and organize your data, including the children's questions and observations after each visit. If there are several adults visiting the tree with you, someone can take notes to help the children remember what they observed and said.

O The investigation may take more than an hour as you will need to: visit the tree, study the tree, and "organize your data" when you return.

## KEY MATH STANDARDS CHILDREN PRACTICE

**Making Connections:** between books and their own observations
**Measuring:** measuring and comparing measurements of the tree
**Representing:** through pictures and graphs of observations

## KEY SCIENCE STANDARDS CHILDREN PRACTICE

**Life Science:** investigating growth and change in nature
**Science as Inquiry:** all the skills, ideas, and processes

## STEP BY STEP

1. Take your group of children on a walk to visit "your" tree. Encourage the children to use their senses to observe and investigate the tree.
   *What do you notice?*
   *What colors do you see? What shapes?*
   *What do you observe under the tree? What do you observe in the tree?*

Look carefully for signs of animal life in and around the tree. These could be squirrels, leaves chewed by insects, birds' nests, and so on. From a short distance, sit and watch the tree quietly. Are there any birds or animals visiting the tree?

Sit and listen quietly. Ask: *What do you hear? Describe the sounds.*

Walk around the tree and stop and smell. Ask: *What do you smell? Describe the smells.*

Touch the tree. Ask children to describe how the tree feels. Use magnifying glasses to study the bark and leaves of the tree.

Ask children to sit and draw the tree. Take a photograph of the tree.

Measure the tree.

When you return to the classroom, use a chart to make a record of Our First Visit to Our Tree in [name of month]. You could include any of the following information on your chart:

- Your observations,
- Questions the children have,
- Predictions about changes you'll notice at next month's visit,
- Your measurement of the tree,
- A leaf sample,
- Information about what you see and find under the tree, and
- Pictures or photographs.

2. In one month visit the tree again. Repeat your investigation and record your data. You may want to add new categories to your chart, including "Changes We Noticed."
3. Visit your tree once a month during the school year. Continue to collect your data, make comparisons, and compile drawings and photographs.
4. Begin a display from the collected observations, drawings, and photos of Our Tree. Talk with the children about the changes you notice.

## Talk with Children

- Encourage "What if?" and "What's that?" questions.
- Encourage the children to use descriptive words as they describe what they see, hear, feel, and smell.
- Encourage the children to use positional words: *over, under, near,* and so on.
- Help the children make predictions about the changes they might see on the next visit to the tree.

**Observe Children**

○ Notice which children automatically touch the tree with their hands and which children tend to observe it from a distance.

○ Encourage children to try new skills. For example, the tactile or hands-on learners could try to explore the bark and leaves with their hands and the visual learners can observe with their eyes and ears and describe what they notice.

○ Which children make connections between what they saw on a previous visit?

○ Do children's drawings capture the changes they see month to month?

○ Which children use descriptive words when they talk about what they observe?

## EXTEND THE LEARNING

○ This investigation will take a full year to complete (or at least several seasons).

## CONNECT WITH FAMILIES

Display photographs of your tree, children's drawings of the tree, and your data collections along with the following:

### Be Friends with a Tree

We're making friends with a tree. We visited the tree for the first time this week and we will visit "our tree" several times this year. By visiting and observing "our tree" we practice:

▣ Making careful observations using our senses and

▣ Collecting information about our observations.
   After we have visited the tree many times we will:

▣ Notice the changes and characteristics of each season and

▣ Make predictions about "our tree" and then check our predictions on the next visit.

# INVESTIGATION: EXPLORING OUTSIDE

Children explore a small area of ground, observing and recording what they see.

## WHAT'S NEEDED
3–5 foot lengths of string or yarn
magnifying glass or other magnifier (optional)

Read a book such as *If You Find a Rock* by Peggy Christian while you do this investigation with the children.

## THINGS TO CONSIDER
O  Make sure there's enough adult supervision for the investigation.

## KEY MATH STANDARDS CHILDREN PRACTICE
**Making Connections:** between books and their own observations
**Representing:** through pictures and graphs of observations

## KEY SCIENCE STANDARDS CHILDREN PRACTICE
**Life Science:** investigating growth and change in nature
**Science as Inquiry:** all the skills, ideas, and processes

## STEP BY STEP
1. Go outside to a safe place where the children can crawl on the ground and explore.
2. Demonstrate how to make the yarn or string into a loop on the grass and have each child make a loop. This loop will define an area for each child to explore.
3. Have the children get down on the ground and explore their areas inside the loops. If you have them, use magnifying glasses  or other magnifiers to look even more closely. Allow plenty of time for observation.
4. Talk with the children about what is inside the loop:
   *What can you see in the grass? How many different creatures do you find?*
   *What does the grass look like up close?*
5. Have the children each represent their areas by drawing a picture and some of the things they saw. Have an adult write down the names, colors, descriptions, and any other detail of the children's observations.

### Talk with Children
O  Encourage the children to use descriptive words as they describe what they see and smell. Encourage them to use positional words, too: *over, under, near*, and so on. What do the children think it would be like to be as small as an insect in the grass?

## Observe Children

○ Do the children's drawings capture what they observed? Which children used descriptive words about what they observed? Did the children use comparative words such as *bigger than*, *smaller than*, and *more than*?

## EXTEND THE LEARNING: MAKE A MINI-ENVIRONMENT

Create individual environments to explore.

## WHAT'S NEEDED

clear plastic container (a plastic salad or deli container works well)
soil
plants like grass or moss
smaller container (optional)
spray bottle of water
sticks and stones

## STEP BY STEP

1. Working together, make a mini-environment. A mini-habitat can have soil, plants like grass or moss, sticks and stones, and perhaps a small container of water for a pond.

2. After gathering the materials, help the children add the soil, seeds or plants, and other natural objects to the container. Use a spray bottle of water to dampen the soil before closing the lid.

3. Have the children observe the mini-environment for changes over time. Suggest that the children draw pictures and tell stories about the changes they see.

## CONNECT WITH FAMILIES

Display the children's drawings, along with the following:

### Exploring Outside

We observed small areas in our backyard and represented our observations with drawings. By observing and representing, we practice:

◘ Making careful observations using our senses, and

◘ Collecting information about our observations.

MATH AND SCIENCE INVESTIGATIONS

# INVESTIGATION: PUDDLES, PUDDLES

Children observe puddles appearing and disappearing (evaporating).

## WHAT'S NEEDED

camera

chalk or string

container for water

puddles from a recent rainstorm

**Note**: The puddle has to be in an area where it won't be disturbed.

Read a book such as *Come on, Rain!* by Karen Hesse with the children while you do this investigation.

## THINGS TO CONSIDER

O  You'll be doing this activity around water, so be sure the children are wearing proper footwear. If it has not rained, pouring water on a flat area will create a puddle.

## KEY MATH STANDARDS CHILDREN PRACTICE

Measuring

Representing data

## KEY SCIENCE STANDARDS CHILDREN PRACTICE

Earth Science: observing how puddles change

Science as Inquiry: asking questions

Science as Inquiry: noticing change over time

## STEP BY STEP

1.  On a rainy day, talk with the children about where rain might come from. Make a list of their ideas.
2.  Talk together about where you have seen puddles form. Are there places nearby where you might find puddles?
3.  After a rainstorm, find an area with puddles on concrete or blacktop. Trace around the puddle with chalk or lay out string along the edge. Take a photograph and note the time you took the picture. Leave the puddle.
4.  Return to check on the puddle after a few hours. What has happened? Encourage the children to trace around the puddle again or move the string. What are some of their ideas about what has happened to the water? Take another picture and note the time.
5.  Try to observe the puddle a couple of times before it totally evaporates. Make puddles again on a hot day and see how fast they evaporate (change from a liquid to a vapor). Take a few more photographs to show the changes.

**Note**: If you don't have an outside area to make puddles, make puddles inside! Fill two containers with water. Cover one container with a lid or a plastic bag. Put both containers in a sunny location. Observe the containers over time and talk about changes that you see.

*What happens to the water in the container with the lid?*
*What happens to the water in the uncovered container?*

> The heat of the sun evaporates the water in a puddle or uncovered dish. A cover on a container stops the water from leaving so water droplets collect on the cover. In the natural cycle, water evaporates and joins the moisture in the air and clouds. Eventually, it becomes rain or other forms of precipitation.

## Talk with Children

○ Encourage discussion about the changes the children notice in the puddles. You might ask:

*Is there more water or less water?*
*What do you think happened to the water?*

○ Be sure to introduce new vocabulary, such as *evaporation, vapor, moisture,* and *precipitation* when the children are ready.

## Observe Children

○ Children are fascinated by how things change. Some changes are almost magical, such as a puddle growing smaller. Notice how they describe this change. Some may say the water disappeared. Ask the children to describe where the water went, as the puddle shrinks. Record the descriptive words children use. Do they make connections to changes in other things they have seen?

## EXTEND THE LEARNING: TRY MAKING IT RAIN!

Making it rain is fun, but also filled with opportunities to learn about science.

## WHAT'S NEEDED

clear plastic container
ice cubes
plate
very hot tap water (adult use only)

## STEP BY STEP

1. Fill the container with very hot tap water. Place the plate on top of the container. After a few minutes, place ice cubes on the plate. What happens?

2. This is similar to what happens outdoors as warm, moist air rises and meets colder temperatures. Water vapor condenses and forms precipitation that falls to the Earth as rain (or snow, sleet, or hail).

## CONNECT WITH FAMILIES

Display photos of the puddles and the changes, along with the following:

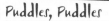

### Puddles, Puddles

We've been observing puddles appearing and disappearing (evaporating). We measured the puddles to show the changes as they occurred. When we did this, we practiced:

- Observing change over time,
- Measuring, and
- Asking scientific questions such as *How did it change?*

# INVESTIGATION: MAKING A WEATHER CHART

Children record weather observations and measurements, noticing patterns and making predictions.

## WHAT'S NEEDED
calendar with large squares
rain gauge
thermometer
weather stickers or rubber stamps

## THINGS TO CONSIDER
○ If you collect data about the weather, it should be part of your daily routine. Making comparisons is a key component of this investigation. Allow the children the opportunity to note the weather information in a chart.

## KEY MATH STANDARDS CHILDREN PRACTICE
**Numbers and Operations:** have a sense of quantity
**Numbers and Operations:** recognize and name written numerals
**Numbers and Operations:** representing and communicating data in a chart

## KEY SCIENCE STANDARDS CHILDREN PRACTICE
**Earth and Space Science:** observe and discuss seasonal and weather patterns
**Earth and Space Science:** using the senses to explore the weather and seasons
**Science as Inquiry:** collect, discuss, and record weather data
**Science as Inquiry:** use observations and data to make predictions
**Science as Inquiry:** use tools to gather weather information

## STEP BY STEP
1. Sit with the children and look at, read, and enjoy lots of books about the weather, such as *In the Rain with Baby Duck* by Amy Hest, *Weather Words and What They Mean* by Gail Gibbons, and *Down Comes the Rain* by Franklyn Branley. Talk with the children about words used to describe weather: *hot, cold, sunny, rainy, humid, cloudy, stormy, thundering, snowing, foggy,* and *windy.* Ask questions such as: *Can you tell by looking out the window at the sky what kind of a day it will be? How do you know?*
2. Work together to make a monthly weather chart and explain that in each date square the children will record their observations.
3. Set aside a time each day when you will record your observations about the current weather and, if possible, the temperature and rainfall. On weekends ask the children to remember what the weather was like on those days.
4. Begin collecting your data with weather stamps and drawings. Talk about how the weather is the same or different from the previous day or previous week.
5. At the end of the month, look at and talk about your chart. Use your weather data for counting and comparing questions such as: *How many sunny days did we have this week?*

MATH AND SCIENCE INVESTIGATIONS

*How many inches of rain fell in that last storm? What do you notice about the temperature? The rainfall?*

6. Save several months' data to make comparisons: Which month(s) had the most rainy days? the most sunny days?

## Talk with Children

O  Make sure all the children participate in this investigation by taking turns recording the data.

O  Have children use descriptive words to describe the weather: *cold, freezing, icy, frigid.*

O  Keep in mind that many picture books have weather themes and introduce new vocabulary as well.

### November

| | | | 1 ☼ 50 | 2 ◎ 50 | 3 ☁ 50 |
|---|---|---|---|---|---|
| 4 ☼ 48 | 5 ☼ 52 | 6 ☁ 44 | 7 ☁ 48 | 8 ☁🌧 37 | 9 ☼ 40 ◎ | 10 ☁🌧 34 |
| 11 ❄ 30 | 12 ☁🌧 48 | 13 ☁ 46 | 14 ☼ 47 ◎ | 15 ☼ 49 | 16 ☁ 45 | 17 ☼ 49 |
| 18 ☁ 37 | 19 ❄ 30 ◎ | 20 ❄ 29 | 21 ❄ 47 ☁ | 22 | 23 | 24 |
| 25 | 26 | 27 | 28 | 29 | 30 | |

## Observe Children

O  Which children are eager to collect data? Do some children already know about weather patterns and make predictions?

---

Use weather data for counting and comparing questions such as:
*How many sunny days did we have this week?*
*How many inches of rain fell in that last storm?*

Discuss and list interesting observations that can be collected about your local weather.
*Are there hurricanes or tornadoes where we live?*
*Is it foggy in the morning and sunny in the afternoon?*

After you begin to collect information there will be many opportunities to look for patterns, make comparisons and predictions.

## EXTEND THE LEARNING: MAKE A RAIN GAUGE!

Use this rain gauge to know exactly how much rain fell.

## WHAT'S NEEDED

clear plastic jar, preferably one with straight sides
markers
paper
ruler

## STEP BY STEP

1. Measure the amount of rain that falls by helping the children make a rain gauge. You'll need a clear jar with straight sides (not curved), a ruler, and paper and markers for recording the results.
2. Place the jar outside, in an open area not too close to buildings or under trees, before it starts to rain.
3. Use the ruler to measure how much rain has been collected in your jar. Record the date and how much rain you collected.
4. Empty the jar after each use.

## CONNECT WITH FAMILIES

Display your weather chart, along with the following:

### Making a Weather Chart

We've been observing the weather and collecting data to represent on our weather chart. We made comparisons and predictions, too! When we did this, we practiced:
O  Observing and discussing weather patterns, and
O  Collecting, recording, and representing weather data.

You'll find many weather activities for young children online or in books for young children. However, as you review these activities, ask yourself:
*Where's the science? Where's the math?*
*Is there intentional use of appropriate vocabulary?*
*Can you match the activity to a math or science standard?*
*Does the activity help children practice the process skills of science?*
*Are there opportunities for data collection? For counting? Recognizing shapes and patterns?*

MATH AND SCIENCE INVESTIGATIONS

# INVESTIGATION: WHAT DO I WEAR WHEN?

Children learn about the weather by talking about and sorting appropriate clothing and accessories for each season.

## WHAT'S NEEDED

chart paper for brainstorming lists
collection of clothing and accessories for all kinds of weather conditions
signs with both words and graphics to post in four areas of the room: For Spring, For Summer, For Autumn, For Winter

Read a book such as *The Snowy Day* by Ezra Jack Keats to explore further the concept of seasons with young children.

## THINGS TO CONSIDER

○ This investigation will work for children of all developmental levels. As you gather clothes and accessories be sure to include items that can be worn or used in more than one season. This will spark interesting conversations.

## KEY MATH STANDARDS CHILDREN PRACTICE

**Communicating:** using pictures as a guide for sorting
**Making Connections:** linking real-life experiences to math experiences

## KEY SCIENCE STANDARDS CHILDREN PRACTICE

**Earth and Space Science:** using knowledge of weather to select appropriate clothing
**Science as Inquiry:** sorting a collection of clothes according to seasons

## STEP BY STEP

1. Ask children:
   *If you were going to the playground on a summer day, what would you wear?*
   *What else would you bring?*
   Give each child an opportunity to answer the question. List all responses on a sheet of chart paper with "What I Wear in the Summer" at the top.
2. Talk with the children about going to the same playground in the winter.
   *What would you wear if it were winter?*
   *What else would you bring?*
   List all responses on a sheet of chart paper with "What I Wear in the Winter" at the top.
3. Repeat this brainstorm for all the seasons in your climate.
4. Set the stage for the movement part of this investigation by marking four areas in the room and place the season signs, one in each area. Move the brainstorm lists to the appropriate area.

5.  Place your collection of clothes and accessories on the floor. Hold up each item and ask children in which season it belongs. When everything has been sorted, mix all the clothes up again and re-sort. Set a timer and challenge children to sort all the items in five minutes or less.

## Talk with Children

O  Ask the children about the clothes and accessories:
   *Why can you wear the same jacket for fall, winter, and spring?*
   *Why are snow boots different from rain boots?*
   Encourage the children to use math and science language as they discuss the attributes of different items: *colder than, warmer than, heavier than, lighter than, over, under.*

O  Brainstorm with the children:
   *How else could you keep warm? keep dry? keep cool?*

O  Ask the children questions about the clothes:
   *How would you feel wearing that in the hot sun?*
   *How would you feel wearing that in a cold wind?*
   *This feels heavy and thick—what season is it for?*

## Observe Children

O  Do the children notice that you can wear some of the same clothes in different seasons?

O  Are the children asking "What if" questions, such as:
   *What if it were summer, but it was raining really hard?*
   *What if you were running around in the snow and got really hot?*

O  When the children decide where a piece of clothing goes, do they try to decide between one or more seasons?

## EXTEND THE LEARNING

O  Help the children make their own *What I Wear in [Season]* books to display and take home. Put together blank books with four or more pages, one for each child. Ask the children to select a season for their books and then to cut out pictures from catalogs and magazines for their books or draw pictures of themselves during the season they select.

## CONNECT WITH FAMILIES

Display the brainstorm lists. You may also want to display your clothing and accessories collection, photographs of children doing the investigation, and the *What I Wear in [Season]* books. Post the following on a bulletin board:

### What Do I Wear When...?

We've been sorting a collection of clothes and accessories by seasons. We practiced:

O  Sorting different clothes by seasons,

O  Using our knowledge of weather to select appropriate clothing, and

O  Sorting a set of clothing based on different attributes.

MATH AND SCIENCE INVESTIGATIONS

# CHAPTER 5

# Shapes and Spaces

As children move around and explore their world, they begin to recognize the differences in the form and location of objects. In this way they are learning basic elements in geometry.

Geometry is the area of mathematics that involves shape, size, position, direction, and movement. The National Council of Teachers of Mathematics says, "As [children] become familiar with shape, structure, location, and transformations and as they develop spatial reasoning, they lay the foundation for understanding not only their spatial world but also other topics in mathematics and in art, science, and social studies."

Young children learn the foundations of geometry by recognizing and naming shapes and forms of familiar objects such as windows, doors, tables, light fixtures, signs, wheels, and buildings. They become aware of the position of objects and describe where objects are located with positional words and phrases, which helps children be more precise with their descriptions and follow directions better. Early geometry experiences help children describe, measure, build, and classify the world around them.

Eventually children develop spatial skills that allow them to form mental pictures of objects' shapes, sizes, and relationships. Children can then learn to use diagrams, drawings, maps, and pictures to understand and represent objects in their world. Understanding geometric shapes is more complex than just knowing the names of common shapes such as circle, square, and triangle. Even very young children explore shapes and spaces in everyday activities:

Ling likes to take puzzles apart and put them back together.

After going on a shape search, Owen exclaims, "Look at all the circles in this room!"

Working at the shapes center, Miguel says, "Look! I made a square with two triangles!"

Caitlin explains how to get to the cafeteria: "You go down the hall past the restroom and turn left by the bulletin board. You walk straight ahead and go through the red doors."

In the play area, children take turns hiding the doll. Ms. Brown asks the children, "Is it under the stove? Is it next to the cradle?"

Children learn geometry best through hands-on experiences. Anything they can touch and manipulate—such as shapes—enhances their understanding.

**Some ideas to start you thinking about math:**

**Idea** As children move around and explore the outside world, they learn a lot about geometry. For young children, geometry begins with recognizing and naming the shapes and forms of familiar objects such as windows, doors, signs, wheels, buildings, trees, and flowers. The position of objects, the relationship of one object to another, and giving and following directions are other important parts of geometry. When children explore outside, they hear and use many positional words, such as *on/off, on top of/under, top/bottom, in front of/behind, next to/between, up/down, forward/ backward/sideways, around/through, near/far,* and *close to/far from.*

**Some ideas to start you thinking about science:**

**Idea** As children investigate shapes they practice many Science as Inquiry skills. They ask questions (What's that? What if?), they collect and use data (recognize and count shapes they see), and communicate information and ideas (through drawings and charts they observe, recognize relationships, and sort and classify).

**Some ideas to start you thinking about language and literacy:**

**Idea** One component of the world that children love to notice as they go places is signs. Learning to interpret the pictures and words on signs is an appropriate and natural early reading experience for young children. Because signs often combine shape, color, pictures, and words to give a message, even very young children discover that they can read signs!

MATH AND SCIENCE INVESTIGATIONS

## VOCABULARY

**angle:** a shape formed by two lines diverging from a common point

**copy:** a thing made to be similar or identical to another

**create:** to bring something into existence

**extend:** to draw or arrange in a given direction

**sequence:** arrange in a particular order

Although most picture books feature shapes as part of their illustrations, here are some shape concept books:

*Mouse Shapes* by Ellen Stoll Walsh

*Round Is a Mooncake: A Book of Shapes* by Roseanne Thong

*Shapes, Shapes, Shapes* by Tana Hoban

*Shape Capers* by Cathryn Falwell

*The Shape of Things* by Dayle Ann Dodds

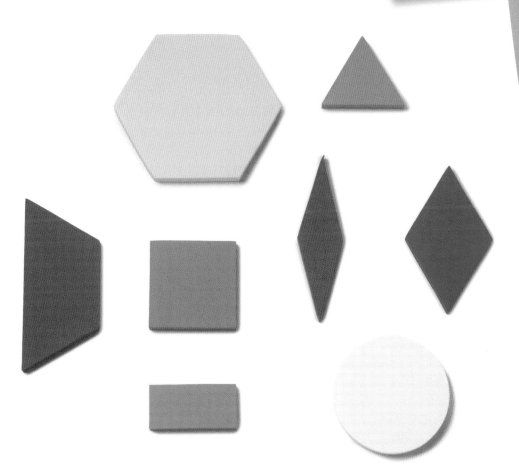

# INVESTIGATION: SHAPE WALK

Children go for a walk in the neighborhood. During that walk they look for and talk about geometric shapes in the environment.

## WHAT'S NEEDED

selection of pattern/attribute shapes

Read a book such as *Shapes all Around* by DK Publishing to introduce shapes to children.

## THINGS TO CONSIDER

O Children will need help in training their eyes to look for shapes. Start by helping them find shapes that are very close, at eye or ground level. Some children will need to trace the outline of a shape with their fingers before they can say what it is. Encourage children to do this.

O You will want to do this investigation many times. Combine the shape walk with other walks.

O Children will find many creative ways to play with shapes. Make them available for daily play.

## KEY MATH STANDARDS CHILDREN PRACTICE

Geometry and Spatial Sense: matching, naming, and describing shapes

## KEY SCIENCE STANDARDS CHILDREN PRACTICE

Science as Inquiry: observing and gathering information when noticing and comparing shapes

## STEP BY STEP

1. Engage the children in a discussion about a particular shape, such as a rectangle. Hold up the rectangle. Ask the children what they notice about the rectangle. Listen for words that describe its shape, size, name, and other attributes.

2. With the children, look carefully around your room for other rectangles. You'll be surprised at how many rectangles you and the children will see—books, ceiling tiles, windows, and other objects and features of the room.

3. Give each child a rectangle. Go on a shape walk. Tell the children you will be looking for rectangles. As you walk, be sure to stop frequently and look all around for rectangles.

4. Repeat this investigation several times, focusing on a single shape each time.

### Talk with Children

O When you see a shape, describe its position to the children. Use positional words such as *over, under, behind, on top of, next to, in front of*, and other spatial words. Encourage the children to use these positional words.

○ Encourage the children to talk about the shapes they see. Ask questions:
*How is that rectangle similar to your pattern block?*
*How are those two triangles different?*

## Observe Children

○ Are the children noticing shapes, but mislabeling them? Praise the children for finding such shapes and let them know the correct name. Show the children the pattern/attribute block that goes with the name.

○ Notice if the children see the shape in a whole structure or just the parts of it. For example, do children notice a circle shape in a church window, or do they notice that the side of the church is one huge rectangle?

○ Do the children use positional words when they show you where a shape is?

## EXTEND THE LEARNING

○ Go on a Shape Search. Try an outdoor shape search. Instead of looking for just one shape, you and the children will try to find and name as many shapes as you can both indoors and outdoors. Keep a list of all the different shapes you see and where you see the shape:
*We saw doors that were rectangles.*
*We saw a sidewalk block that was a square.*

## CONNECT WITH FAMILIES

○ Display shapes, photographs of shapes you saw on your walk, and observations the children made on the shape walk.

○ Post the following on your bulletin board:

Shape Walk
We went on a Shape Walk. We all looked for the same shape—circles, triangles, rectangles, squares, or other shapes.
We kept track of how many shapes we found. On our Shape Walk, we practiced:
• Matching, naming, and describing basic shapes,
• Learning about the characteristics of the basic shapes,
• Gathering information from the environment, and
• Using positional words such as *over, under, near, next to*, and so on

Almost any picture book offers opportunities to talk about and explore shapes. Here are a few suggestions:
*The Very Hungry Caterpillar* by Eric Carle (circles)
*Knuffle Bunny* by Mo Willems (different shapes on every page)
*Every Friday* by Dan Yaccarino (different shapes on every page)
*The Great Fuzz Frenzy* by Susan Stevens Crummel and Janet Stevens (circles)
*Hippos Go Berserk!* by Sandra Boynton (squares and rectangles)

# INVESTIGATION: THE SHAPE OF ART

In this investigation children create designs and pictures out of paper shapes.

## WHAT'S NEEDED
colored paper
crayons or marker
cut-out shapes
glue
rulers
pattern/attribute shapes
scissors

Read a book such as *The Wing on a Flea* by Ed Emberley to introduce shapes in art to children.

## THINGS TO CONSIDER
O  This is an open-ended opportunity for children to design and experiment with shapes. Children will make designs and shapes of all kinds.

## KEY MATH STANDARDS CHILDREN PRACTICE
**Communicating:** telling others about math-related work and using math language—numbers, shape names, size words, location language
**Geometry and Spatial Sense:** combining shapes to make designs that have symmetry and balance
**Geometry and Spatial Sense:** matching, sorting, naming, and describing basic shapes
**Geometry and Spatial Sense:** understanding and using words that describe the location of objects

## KEY SCIENCE STANDARDS CHILDREN PRACTICE
**Science as Inquiry:** asking scientific questions such as "What if I put this shape here?" or "How many shapes do I need for this house?"
**Science as Inquiry:** recognizing patterns and relationships as children experiment with shape designs

## STEP BY STEP
1.  Playing with Shapes
Encourage the children to play with a variety of shapes and watch how they experiment with the shapes as they make designs and pictures. You will probably notice them doing many things with the shapes. For example, the children might:
O  Put two triangles together to make a diamond,
O  Build a tower of hexagons,

- Make a wall by standing the shapes on edge side-by-side,
- Fit a circle inside a square,
- Make a person or tree or house, or
- Make a pattern, alternating rectangles and triangles.

2. Making Art with Shapes

After ample free play with shapes, suggest creating "shape pictures" with paper shapes and glue.

Provide a large selection of precut shapes in lots of different sizes and colors. Also, make paper, rulers, and scissors available for children to draw and cut out their own shapes.

Give the children time to experiment with arranging the shapes on a large piece of paper or cardboard.

As the children create designs, give them glue so they can stick the shapes in place.

## Talk with Children

- Model calling the shapes by their proper names.
- Encourage the children to talk about the shapes by asking:
  *What do you notice about the triangle?*
- Encourage the children to compare shapes by asking "What's the same?" and "What's different?" questions.
- You can help the children make connections by asking:
  *What does your picture remind you of?*
- Teach the children what symmetry is by pointing out the symmetrical parts of their designs. Model the words *symmetry* and *symmetrical*.
- Give the children opportunities to use location language such as *over, under, above, below, beside, next to, near,* and *far* by talking about the placement of shapes on their collages.

## Observe Children

- How do the children put shapes together to makes pictures or designs? (intentionally? randomly? do they copy from *The Shape of Things*?)
- What do you notice about the children's use of shapes? (use one primary shape? use many different shapes? put shapes together to make other shapes?)
- How do the children organize their collages? (symmetrical designs? patterns? clustering similar shapes together?)
- How do the children talk about their shape collages? (by naming the shapes? by comparing the designs to other things: *It looks like a spaceship!* by counting the shapes in their collage? by thinking aloud?)

## EXTEND THE LEARNING: SHAPE PICTURES AND DESIGNS

### WHAT'S NEEDED
cut-out paper shapes or sticker shapes for pictures
foam shapes for exploration

### STEP BY STEP

1. Encourage the children to explore a variety of shapes and watch how the children experiment with the shapes as they make designs and pictures. As they work alone or in small groups, ask questions such as:

   *What is the name of this shape?*
   *What's the same and what's different about this shape from that one?*
   *What shapes can you make by combining two or more shapes?*

2. Challenge the children to make their own pictures using either the sticker shapes or gluing cut-out paper shapes on pieces of paper. Ask questions such as:

   *How many different shapes did you use in your picture?*
   *How many shapes are there altogether in your design?*

MATH AND SCIENCE INVESTIGATIONS

# EXTEND THE LEARNING: STRING SHAPES

## WHAT'S NEEDED

chenille sticks (optional)
glue or tape
poster board or construction paper
string, cut into manageable lengths
toothpicks (optional)

## STEP BY STEP

1. Using pieces of pre-cut string, the children can make a variety of shapes. Tape or glue the shapes to a piece of poster board or construction paper.
2. The children can identify the shapes as an adult helper labels each shape. The children may also use chenille sticks or toothpicks to make the shapes.

# EXTEND THE LEARNING: SHAPE COLLAGE

## WHAT'S NEEDED

magazines and other sources of pictures
paper
scissors
tape or glue

## STEP BY STEP

○ Have the children find and cut out examples of one shape or examples of different shapes and use the shapes to make a collage.

# EXTEND THE LEARNING: JUST ONE SHAPE

Compare shapes when they are moved, flipped, or turned.

## WHAT'S NEEDED

crayons or markers
paper
scissors

## STEP BY STEP

1. Have the children decide which shape they'd like to use.
2. Demonstrate how one shape, drawn in different sizes and forms, can be used to make a one-shape picture: a town made out of triangles, a space ship from rhombi (diamond shapes), a room from rectangles, and so on.
3. Help the children draw and cut out the shapes and then create their one-shape pictures. Talk together about the many ways just one shape can be made: small, big, elongated, and so on.

4. Challenge the children to make a picture using as many different shapes as possible.

## EXTEND THE LEARNING: MY SHAPE BOOK
The children find shapes from various sources and use them to illustrate a book.

## WHAT'S NEEDED
bookmaking materials including paper, scissors, glue, crayons, and markers
shapes to trace
magazines and other sources of pictures

## STEP BY STEP
1. Have the children select one shape and illustrate the pages of a blank book with objects illustrating the shape. Pictures can be cut from magazines or drawn by each child.
2. The book itself may be made in a shape. For example, rectangle-shaped pieces of paper for rectangles, paper plates for circles, and so on.

## CONNECT WITH FAMILIES
Display children's shape art and examples of various shapes with the following information:

### The Shape of Art
We made designs and pictures out of shapes. When we were doing this we practiced:
O Naming different shapes and
O Combining shapes to make other shapes and designs.

As the children learn to recognize shapes, they can also learn to use words to describe the shape. This enriches their understanding of the shape itself and they learn new vocabulary. So, for example, a *square* is a figure with four equal sides and four right angles.

Children won't need to memorize all these words to understand squareness, but it's important to introduce and use terms like *angle* and *equal*, even with young children. Once you've introduced the words, make sure to use them whenever it's appropriate.

## CHAPTER 6

# Exploring Spaces (and Places!)

It is easy to use positional and directional words with children during everyday activities: acting out stories, talking about art projects, designing and using treasure maps or in scavenger hunts, in conversations about trips and transportation.

One way to introduce and talk about maps (spatial thinking) is to use a concept book such as *Me on the Map*. As with many concept books, you will want to look at and read just one or two spreads at different times and make connections to the other books you've read and discussed.

However, any book about taking a walk or going on a trip offers opportunities to talk about maps, mapping, and giving or following directions. Here are a few suggestions:
*Me on the Map* by Joan Sweeney
*As the Crow Flies* by Gail Hartman
*My Map Book* by Sara Fanellli
*Jonathan and His Mommy* by Irene Smalls
*Down the Road* by Alice Schertle

Some ideas to get you thinking about math:

**Idea**    For young children, learning about shapes leads naturally to developing their spatial sense. Both shapes and spaces are contained in the Geometry and Spatial Sense content standard. Try to encourage children to talk about trips they've taken, how they got to school that day, where their grandparents live. Any time a child describes where something is located, he is practicing that standard.

Some ideas to get you thinking about science:

**Idea**    Asking lots of scientific questions and promoting inquiry in general is important in your everyday activities with children. When children talk about locations and directions, they're recognizing relationships between and among objects and places.

Some ideas to get you thinking about language and literacy:

**Idea**    As children name and describe locations and positions, encourage vocabulary development by listing all of the position words they say: *around, through, beside, under, over,* and so on. The more precise vocabulary they use, the better they can describe where an object or a place is!

### Locational and Directional Words

| | |
|---|---|
| on, off | up/down |
| on top of/under | forward/backward/sideways |
| top/bottom | around/through |
| in front of/behind | near/far |
| next to/between | close to/far from |

## VOCABULARY

**destination:** the place where someone or something is going

**directions:** instructions for how to reach a destination

**landmark:** an object or feature that enables someone to establish their location

**location:** a particular place or position

**map:** the graphic representation of an area

**position:** the place where an object or person is located

**route:** the way or course taken in getting from a starting place to a destination

**MATH AND SCIENCE INVESTIGATIONS**

## Act Out a Story

Acting out stories, folktales, original stories, or poems provides children with opportunities to hear and practice using positional and directional words and to follow directions.

Traditional folktales such as *The Three Billy Goats Gruff, Jack and the Beanstalk,* and *Little Red Riding Hood* (as well as modern stories such as *Rosie's Walk* by Pat Hutchins) provide opportunities for using directional and positional words.

When children act out words such as *over, under, near,* and *far* they are learning about location, space, and shape. They learn about numbers when they take *two small steps* and *one giant step.* Older children will be able to understand ideas such as *turn left* and *turn right.*

# INVESTIGATION: TELL ME HOW TO GET THERE

In this investigation, you and the children describe how to find a hidden treasure.

## WHAT'S NEEDED

objects to be the treasure such as a shiny penny, a beautiful shell, or a special stone

A book such as *Rosie's Walk* by Pat Hutchins is a great book to read with the children while you do this investigation.

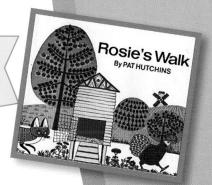

## THINGS TO CONSIDER

○ You may need to start with very simple hiding places and simple directions.
○ As you give directions use as many descriptive words as you can. Use action words like *sneak* or *slide.* Include adverbs like *slowly* or *quickly.* Be sure to use plenty of positional words!

## KEY MATH STANDARDS CHILDREN PRACTICE

**Communicating:** using the math language of location and size
**Geometry and Spatial Sense:** understanding and using words that describe where objects are located
**Measuring:** understanding and using measurement words

## KEY SCIENCE STANDARDS CHILDREN PRACTICE

**Science as Inquiry:** observing and gathering information by listening to and giving directions

## STEP BY STEP

1. Talk with the children about the reasons we give someone directions. You may want to tell them that directions are instructions telling us how to do something or how to get somewhere.

2. Ask the children to close their eyes while you hide the object. Choose one child to find the hidden object. Have that child ask, "Where should I go?" As you give that child directions, use as many descriptive words as you feel the child can understand. An example might be as follows:
   *Stand up. Take giant steps forward until you get to the edge of the green rug. Tiptoe slowly past the shelf. Look down on the floor next to the desk.*

3. Hide objects in different locations and give all the children an opportunity to follow directions to locate the objects.

4. Repeat the investigation by allowing each child a turn to hide an object and give directions to another child. Be sure that everyone has a chance to be a hider/direction giver.

### Talk with Children

○ Support the children as they learn the meaning of positional words. For example, children often don't know the exact meaning of *next to, behind, above,* or *beside.* Use these words in your daily interactions with children.

### Observe Children

○ Notice how many different words the children use when giving directions. When children can use a word correctly, this is called *expressive vocabulary.*
○ Notice which words the children seem to understand but don't use while speaking. When children can understand a word, but don't use it, it is called *receptive vocabulary.*
○ Notice which children use new vocabulary in their play.

MATH AND SCIENCE INVESTIGATIONS

## EXTEND THE LEARNING

○ Help the children build a very simple obstacle course. Make sure that it is designed so you can use words such as: *over, under, through, around, behind, beside, between, above,* and *below.* Let children test the obstacle course. Perhaps it will be as simple as stepping over a block and then going under the table. Ask the children to add one new element at a time to the obstacle course. For example: step over the block, go under the table, and then take four steps.

○ Use a blanket or large towel to make a tunnel or set up two cardboard boxes on end with another piece of cardboard acting as a roof.

○ Children can draw maps of the obstacle course.

## CONNECT WITH FAMILIES

○ Display the objects used as the treasure, a list of places where the treasure was hidden, and some of the instructions children gave each other.

○ Post the following on your bulletin board:

### Tell Me How to Get There

We've been doing an investigation by following directions. One of us hides a "treasure" and then gives someone else directions on how to find it. While we did this investigation, we practiced:

○ Using words that describe where objects are located,

○ Counting the number of steps we needed to take (for example, turn around and take four steps), and

○ Following step-by-step directions.

# INVESTIGATION: KNOW YOUR NEIGHBORHOOD (MAKING A MAP)

In this investigation you and your group will make simple map pictures that tell a story about getting from one place to another.

## WHAT'S NEEDED

construction paper
glue
markers
scissors
tape

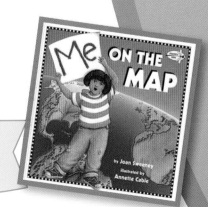

Read *Me on the Map* by Joan Sweeney as you explore making maps with the children.

## THINGS TO CONSIDER

○ In the weeks leading up to this investigation, have maps available in the classroom. The tourist "maps" that show restaurants and landmarks are easy for children to understand.

○ Plan an interesting and safe walking route.

○ Some children may know where objects should go on the map, but may not be able to draw them. They may want to use pictures from magazines to complete their maps.

○ For children with communication challenges, you may need to use actual photographs of the places on the walk to help them understand that the map represents a place they are familiar with.

## KEY MATH STANDARDS CHILDREN PRACTICE

**Geometry and Spatial Sense:** using words to describe where objects are located or how to get somewhere

**Representing:** using pictures to represent object or places

## KEY SCIENCE STANDARDS CHILDREN PRACTICE

Science as Inquiry: collecting and using data by thinking about and drawing what they observe

Science as Inquiry: communicating information and ideas by using drawings to tell others what they have learned.

---

Children learn how to get from one place to another, how to give and follow directions, and how to make and follow a map by:

○ Observing and talking about landmarks,

○ Constructing and understanding information about a route (a connected series of landmarks), and

○ Placing many routes and locations together into a kind of mental map.

---

## STEP BY STEP

1. Engage the children in a conversation about maps. What do they already know about maps? Explain that a map is a picture of a certain area and that some maps help us get from one place to another place.

2. Take a short walk with your group. Stop often and encourage the children to look at and talk about the landmarks they see: buildings, trees, signs, and so on. Make a list of their observations.

3. When you return to the classroom talk together about what you saw, using descriptive and positional words: "the blue house was next to the store with the sign above the door." Review the descriptions of what you saw and add these descriptions to your list.

4. Tape four pieces of construction paper together, or use a roll of newsprint, to make a really large piece of paper. Talk and work together to draw a map of what you saw on the walk. Use drawings, cutouts, or three-dimensional objects to

show buildings, trees, signs, and any other landmarks the children noticed on the walk.

5. When the map is completed, have the children give each other directions, using the map as a guide.

## Talk with Children

O As you walk in the community, point out landmarks you want the children to remember for their maps. You might say:

*Oh, we are on a bridge again. This road goes over the brook twice.*

*Look how close the school really is to the soccer field.*

O Remind the children of things they saw on the walk. You might say something like:

*I see you put the trees next to the post office. I also remember that there was a parking lot next to the post office. What else do you remember was near the post office?*

O When the children make drawings of objects or landmarks that you don't recognize, ask them what they are and label them—always respect the intent of their drawings.

O Encourage the children to share any personal experience they have with the area you are mapping. For example, the children may play in the area or walk this same route with their families.

### Observe Children

- Notice if the children are using some of the language of mapmaking and travel in their free play, words like *leads to, next to, past, over, under, across from, near,* and *far*.
- Are the children interested in drawing more maps on their own?
- Are the children using the block area to continue making maps?

## EXTEND THE LEARNING

- Challenge the children to make their own maps. Go for another walk following the same route. Talk together about what you notice. Allow the children plenty of time to make maps.
- Think about other mapping opportunities such as:
- Using maps when building with blocks or other materials,
- Making maps of fanciful or imaginary places, and
- Making a map of a room, yard, or playground.

## CONNECT WITH FAMILIES

Display the maps and post the following on your bulletin board:

### Know Your Neighborhood

We've been learning how to make maps. In order to "know the neighborhood," we went on a walk and made maps of where we went. We learned that maps are special pictures that represent a place. When we made maps, we practiced:

- Communicating information in writing, and
- Using spatial words such as *around*, *next to*, and *behind*.

# CHAPTER 7

# What Comes Next?

Patterns are things or events that repeat. Having a strong sense of what comes next or what happens next is critically important in mathematics and science. For example, all counting is a sequence. Whether you count forward or backward, by 2s, 5s, or 10s, you have to know what comes next. Pattern recognition is the first step in understanding how our world is constructed and how it functions.

People who work with young children know that following a consistent daily schedule and frequently reviewing it with children is good practice. When children know the sequence of events and are able to predict what happens next, they feel in control, confident, and powerful. Some children constantly ask, "What do we do next?" These children haven't internalized the sequence of the day. They don't want to be surprised by the unexpected.

In addition to having a positive effect on a child's psychological well-being, a strong sense of sequence and pattern has a positive influence on their mental or cognitive growth as well. Understanding and creating sequences, putting things in order, noticing cause-and-effect relationships, and detecting organized patterns are all higher level thinking skills.

Young children thrive when they have a good grasp of what happens next. Here are some examples:

Emma's father is reading *The Doorbell Rang* to her. After he reads, "Nobody makes cookies like Grandma," she says, "I know what's next! The doorbell rings!"

Juan is picked up from his school around the same time each day, usually near the end of an outside recess. After playing for a while, he regularly goes to the fence and asks, "Is Mommy coming now?"

Ms. Mattie and a small group of young children are making cookies, a regular Friday morning event. The recipe is written in words and pictures and is posted on a nearby wall. Lucia is one step ahead of the group. Before the butter and sugar are mixed together, she opens the canister of flour and gets the measuring cup and sifter from the shelf. She asks, "It's time to sift the flour, right?"

Matt has taken a stack of nesting boxes from the shelf. He sits on the floor and begins removing each nested box one by one. As he takes out each box, he places it on the floor and then puts the next one beside it. Pretty soon the six boxes are lined up in order from smallest to largest. Leaving the largest box where it is but turning it upside down, he then places the next smaller box upside down on top of the largest one. He proceeds until he has created a tower of boxes that has the largest one on the bottom and the smallest one on the top.

**Some ideas to start you thinking about math:**

**Idea** Having a strong sense of what happens next is critically important in mathematics. Think about counting. Numbers follow a very predictable sequence that children begin learning at a very young age, often before they are two years old. There are many different ways to count, and as children get older, being able to count backward as well as forward is important. Learning to count in groups—by 2s, 5s, and 10s—is another important counting skill. All counting is a sequence; you have to know what comes next!

Some ideas to start you thinking about science:

**Idea** The question "What happens next?" encourages predicting in any investigation or discussion. All of this predicting can encourage thoughtful, step-by-step work. It can also bring out children's creative ideas about what questions they might like to explore next and how they might do that.

Some ideas to start you thinking about language and literacy:

**Idea** Certain words are used frequently as people engage in sequencing or ordering activities. It is important for children to hear and use words, such as *next, last, smallest, biggest, least, most, shortest, tallest, before,* and *after*. Ordinal number words are also important—*first, second, third,* and so on. Another important link to language and literacy relates to sequence in stories. Predicting what will happen next in stories and recalling the sequence of events are both keys to reading comprehension.

## VOCABULARY

**design:** a pattern or shape, sometimes repeated, used for decoration
**pattern:** repeated organization of objects, sounds, or events

Many picture books feature visual patterns in their illustrations and words. Here are a few suggestions:
*Pattern Fish* by Trudy Harris
*Max Found Two Sticks* by Brian Pinkney
*Lots and Lots of Zebra Stripes* by Stephen R. Swinburne
*Jonathan and His Mommy* by Irene Smalls
*The Little Red Hen* by Margot Zemach

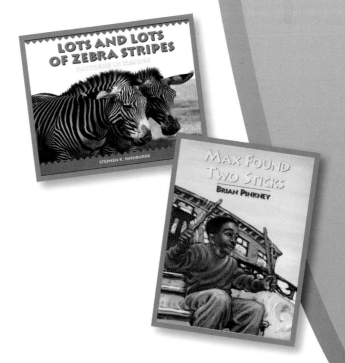

# INVESTIGATION: COPYCAT PATTERNS

In this investigation, you and your group create patterns with blocks and other objects. Children learn to look carefully at someone else's pattern and to copy that pattern.

## WHAT'S NEEDED

collection of objects such as colored blocks, linking cubes, toy trucks, buses, and wooden or plastic shapes

Introduce verbal patterns to the children by reading a book such as *Bein' with You this Way* by W. Nikola-Lisa.

## THINGS TO CONSIDER

○ Patterns are the sequenced or repeated organization of objects, sounds, or events. Use the word *pattern* often with children as you do this investigation. When grouping children for "Copycat Patterns," think about the children's past experiences with pattern play.

## KEY MATH STANDARDS CHILDREN PRACTICE

**Communicating:** telling others about their math-related work and describing patterns by using shape and size words

**Patterns, Functions, and Algebra:** identifying, copying, and making simple patterns

**Patterns, Functions, and Algebra:** using patterns to predict what will come next in a simple pattern

## KEY SCIENCE STANDARDS CHILDREN PRACTICE

**Science as Inquiry:** finding patterns

**Science as Inquiry:** predicting what will come next in a pattern

Most of the world, both natural and human made, is constructed of units that repeat themselves into patterns. If you look closely at living things and human-made things, you will see many examples of single or core units making a simple, single repeating pattern (A-A-A-A-A-A and so on).

The core of patterns can be more complex when different units are added, such as A-B, A-B, A-B, and so on, or A-B-C, A-B-C, A-B-C, and so on.

When listening to music, children can identify rhythm patterns and word patterns in lyrics. Poetry is full of metrical patterns and dance can contain motion patterns.

MATH AND SCIENCE INVESTIGATIONS

## STEP BY STEP

1. Engage the children in a discussion about patterns by looking for patterns on clothing, in the room, or in a book. Begin by pointing out a pattern. You might say:
   *I see a pattern on Conner's shirt. Red square, yellow circle, red square, yellow circle… what comes next?*

2. Place the blocks and other objects on a table. Continue your discussion of patterns by showing the children how to make a pattern by taking objects and arranging them in a sequence or a repeating way. For example,
   *red, blue, yellow; red, blue, yellow; red…*
   *truck, car, car; truck, car, car; truck…*

3. Challenge one child or group of children to identify patterns as you make them. Ask the children to make predictions about what shape or object will come next in a pattern.

4. Once making patterns becomes easier, suggest playing "Copycat Patterns." One child makes a pattern, then another copies the pattern. Be sure that everyone has many experiences making and copying patterns. Encourage the children to think of as many different patterns as possible.

## Talk with Children

○ Encourage the children to talk about their patterns. Ask:
   *What is your sequence?*
   *How can you make a pattern different by adding more colors, shapes, textures?*
○ Encourage the children to look at and describe each other's patterns.

## Observe Children

○ Which children sort first and then make pattern rows? Do some children skip the sorting stage?
○ How do the children decide which shape comes next in their pattern? Is it by saying the pattern aloud or by looking and thinking? Do some ask you or a friend?
○ How do different children copy their partners' patterns? Do they copy it exactly? Do they add extra shapes? Do they leave some shapes out?
○ Listen to the children as they make patterns with shapes. Are the children naming the shapes they are using for their patterns? Do some children chant their patterns (*square, square, circle, square, square, circle, square, square…*) as they build them?

## EXTEND THE LEARNING: PATTERN STRIPS

○ Help the children make pattern strips using different colored squares of paper. When each child is satisfied with the pattern, help him or her glue the squares onto another piece of paper to take home. As the children complete their strips, ask:

*What do you notice about the patterns you made?*
*How are they the same or different?*

○ Help the children listen for and notice language patterns when reading books and poems. For example, say:

*When Papa Bear looks into his bowl, he says, "Someone's been eating my porridge." When Momma Bear looks into her bowl, she says, "Someone's been eating my porridge." And when Baby Bear looks into his bowl, he says,... (What happens next?)*

## EXTEND THE LEARNING: CLAPPING PATTERNS
Children repeat and extend clapping patterns and create new patterns.

## WHAT'S NEEDED
hands

## STEP BY STEP
1. Clap a simple rhythm for the children. Talk about the elements of the pattern: for example, one loud and two soft, or two fast and one loud. Ask them to repeat the pattern. Add another rhythm to the sequence. Ask the children to repeat it.
2. Ask the children to volunteer to create a clapping pattern. Have one child demonstrate the pattern and describe it. Ask the other children to repeat the pattern.
3. When the children can repeat a simple pattern, you might ask one child to clap a pattern and another child to add to it. Continue adding on patterns as long as the children can follow the clapping patterns, probably no more than two or three extensions.

4. Show the children how to represent a clapping pattern. Explain that if we want to write down and remember our patterns we can use foam shapes to show our clapping patterns. For example, one loud and two fast claps could be represented as one square and two triangles.

5. Encourage the children to make a picture of a clapping pattern and then clap it. You can explain that music is written with a pattern of symbols.

When we walk, when we sway to and fro to music, or when we learn to dance, we are engaged in a movement pattern. We are repeating a movement or a combination of movements. The pattern of movement may relate to the music we are moving in time to or the pattern may relate to a set of directions, such as "Hop, hop, skip."

Many children's games involve movement and rhythm—following steps to a dance, learning a skipping song, bouncing a ball and counting, clapping to a song. Children love to repeat a physical skill over and over in the process of learning and internalizing a pattern of movement. Repeated experience with movement helps children build more elaborate and increasingly flexible skills that can be applied to new situations.

Combining movement and rhythm is an effective way of engaging children in learning because it is an active and fun way to internalize patterns. All of this helps children recognize movement patterns in the world around them and adds to their understanding of the way things work.

## EXTEND THE LEARNING: MOVEMENT PATTERNS
Children create and copy movement patterns.

## WHAT'S NEEDED
*Jonathan and His Mommy* by Irene Smalls, *Hop Jump* by Ellen Stoll Walsh, or any book in which the characters move in one or more patterns
paper and markers for recording patterns

## STEP BY STEP
1. Talk with the children about the movement patterns in the book you've selected. Describe some of the movements, such as one big step, two small steps, jump, skip.

2. Ask one child to create and demonstrate a movement pattern such as one BIG step, three small steps, one BIG step, three small steps. Have the children follow each other around the room using this pattern.

3. Show the children how you can record the movement pattern to be able to do it again. Represent the movement pattern using symbols for each type of movement. For example, a hop can be a triangle and a jump can be a circle.

4. Ask the children to create another movement pattern.

5. As the children become comfortable with two-part movement patterns, extend the patterns. For example, step, hop, hop; step, hop, hop; and so on.

Hop  Hop  Jump  Hop  Hop  Jump

### EXTEND THE LEARNING: TAPPING PATTERNS

Children learn to describe and repeat sound patterns using sticks.

### WHAT'S NEEDED

spoons, chopsticks, rhythm sticks, dowels, or other sticks with blunt ends

**Note**: Let the children know what your "stop" signal is, like raising your hand or putting your sticks on the floor. Let them know how they can tap with the sticks, such as tapping the sticks together or gently tapping the floor or a table.

### STEP BY STEP

1. Demonstrate a pattern of taps and have a child describe it. You can do this a few times. One pattern might be two fast taps, two slow taps, and so on.

2. Hand out sticks to the children and allow a few minutes for them to practice tapping them together.

3. Tap a simple rhythm and have the children repeat it. Start very simply. You might want to just start with tap-tap and have the children repeat back, tap-tap. You can then add on more taps, or vary the speed of the taps. You could work up to a variety of tapping fast and tapping slow.

4. Let the children take turns creating a tapping pattern that the other children repeat.

5. Read a book such as *Max Found Two Sticks* by Brian Pinkey, then talk with the children about sound patterns they hear every day—the patterns of rain on a window, the ticking of a clock, birdcalls, or a train whistle. Have the children create a pattern as a sound effect to accompany your reading or playing some music.

6. As the children become comfortable with repeating a pattern, try extending a pattern. For example: One child does tap-tap. The next child repeats tap-tap and adds tap…tap. This can go on as long as the children can remember the sequence, perhaps up to three or four extensions.

MATH AND SCIENCE INVESTIGATIONS

## EXTEND THE LEARNING: PATTERN WALK

Children look for and describe patterns they find while out for a walk in the neighborhood.

## WHAT'S NEEDED

pencils, pens, or markers
clipboards

## STEP BY STEP

1. Engage the children in a discussion about patterns. Remind them that a pattern is something that repeats.
2. Look around the room and ask:
   *What patterns do you see in this room?*
   *How would you describe this pattern?*
   *What comes next in the pattern?*
3. Go on a Pattern Walk. Tell the children they will be looking for patterns on buildings, in nature, on the ground, and so on.
4. As you walk, stop frequently and talk about the patterns you see.
   *How would you describe this pattern?*
   *What comes next in the pattern?*
5. Have the children draw or make notes about the patterns they see. When you return from your Pattern Walk, the children can take their "pattern notes" home.
6. If children have found and noted many patterns, they could make a Patterns Book to take home.

## CONNECT WITH FAMILIES

Display blocks and other "pattern materials" and some patterns created by children along with the following information:

### Copycat Patterns

We've been making patterns and copying each other's patterns. One of us creates a pattern and then asks, "What happens next?" Another tries to recognize and create the same pattern.

While we were doing this we practiced:
• Making and recognizing patterns,
• Predicting what will come next in a pattern, and
• Using mathematical words like *pattern* and *repeating patterns*.

# INVESTIGATION: WHAT'S THE SEQUENCE?

In this investigation, children act out their basic daily routines.

## WHAT'S NEEDED
blank index cards
marker

> Reading a book about bedtime routines such as *10 Minutes till Bedtime* by Peggy Rathmann is a great way to introduce sequences to young children.

## THINGS TO CONSIDER
O  You'll want to begin this investigation as a whole group activity that you narrate.

## KEY MATH STANDARDS CHILDREN PRACTICE
**Patterns, Functions, and Algebra:** acting out and recognizing sequences

## KEY SCIENCE STANDARDS CHILDREN PRACTICE
**Science as Inquiry:** finding patterns by seeing and understanding how one thing influences another

## STEP BY STEP
1. With your group, look at and talk about the bedtime routine in *10 Minutes till Bedtime*.
   Ask the children to retell the boy's bedtime routine. As the children talk, they can point out details from the illustrations in the book.
2. Ask the group to act out each stage of the bedtime routine together: brushing teeth, changing into pajamas, reading a story, taking a bath, going to the toilet, putting pajamas back on, getting a drink, getting into bed, kissing goodnight, and going to sleep.
3. Go around the circle and ask the children for an activity that they do regularly (such as brushing their teeth). Write the activity down on a card and draw a stick figure representation of the action on the card. Point out to the children that the stick figure is one way to "read" the words on the card, and that this figure is another way of writing. Create at least one different routine card for each child.
4. Give everyone a turn choosing a card and acting it out while the other children try to guess what the activity is.
5. Each card represents one activity. Use several cards to create a sequence, such as putting on shoes, putting on a coat, and then walking the dog. Give the children a turn to act out entire sequences—even the sequence of an entire day. While they do this, other children can guess the activities being acted out.

### Talk with Children

- You may need to prompt the children as they act out a daily routine.
- Encourage the children to talk about many different routines: getting ready for school, cooking dinner, going shopping, getting ready for lunch, reading a book, and so on.
- Comment on the individual differences in the same routine:

  *José kisses his dad before he brushes his teeth and Madison kisses her dad after she brushes her teeth.*

  *Brianna eats her breakfast before she gets dressed in the morning, but Jacob gets right out of bed, takes off his pajamas, and puts his play clothes on before breakfast.*
- Talk about the different routines on weekends and holidays.

### Observe Children

- This investigation uses a different type of skill—using body movement to communicate rather than using words. Some children actually remember things better with their bodies and movement than they do by hearing, seeing, or speaking words. This is called *kinesthetic memory*.
- Do you see some children who can remember a long routine by acting it out, but can't verbalize the same thing? They may be kinesthetic learners.
- Do some children just copy the routines of others?
- Are some children eager to act out every routine?
- Can some children easily "read" the routine card?

## EXTEND THE LEARNING: WHAT HAPPENS NEXT?

- After you read any book to children several times, talk about the sequence of events in the story.

  *What happened first in the story?*

  *What happened next?*
- Continue asking questions so that children have many opportunities to think about sequences.
- You may want to give prompts as you discuss the sequence or look at the pictures as you talk or even reread the book.

## CONNECT WITH FAMILIES

Display the "What's the Sequence?" cards. Post the following on your bulletin board:

### What's the Sequence?

We talked about the sequences of our daily routines such as getting ready for bed or going to school in the morning. We made cards that show everyday actions and played a "What's the Sequence?" game of charades. We practiced: Identifying patterns and sequences in everyday situations,

- Using nonverbal communication,
- "Reading" pictures that show actions, and
- Using sequencing words like *first*, *next*, *then*, and *finally*.

# CHAPTER 8

# Growing and Changing

Growth and change are everywhere. They happen all the time. They are inevitable.

When we begin to think about growth and change, we quickly realize how huge this topic is. One way to begin organizing our thoughts about growth and change is to consider different categories.

Some growth and change happen because of people. People change food when they cook and eat it. The environment and neighborhoods change and grow when people build roads, dams, and houses. People change a sheep's fleece into yarn. A person can change a tree into a piece of paper or into a building. People can change a pile of blocks into all sorts of structures.

Other kinds of growth and change are natural. The weather changes from day to day and through the seasons. Caterpillars change into butterflies. Seeds change as they grow into plants. People begin as babies, grow and change into children, and then into adults.

Growth and change may happen very slowly, or much more quickly. A cactus will grow slowly, while a bean sprout will grow quickly. Change can go around in cycles such as the seasons. Some changes are irreversible. Some, such as temperature or weight change, can be measured. Others, such as the change from cookie dough to cookies, can be described but not so easily measured.

Young children are fascinated by growth and change, perhaps because they themselves are growing and changing in so many ways. They notice and talk about this many times each day. Consider these examples:

Alejandro planted bean seeds in his classroom. First thing each morning, he checks his cup of seeds to see if anything has happened overnight; and before he goes home each afternoon, he checks it again!

Mei-Mei tells her friends about her pet. "It's still a baby, so it's a kitten. When it grows up, it'll be a cat."

When Tia's teacher notices her new sneakers, Tia explains, "My feet got too big for my old red ones. I gave them to my little cousin."

Noah is working in the sandbox. His teacher asks, "What are you working on, Noah?" He replies, "At first it was just a little pile of sand, and then it was a mountain. Now I'm making it into a castle."

**Some ideas to start you thinking about math:**

**Idea** As children observe and talk about change, they practice important math skills. Some change involves numbers, such as changing from being five years old to being six years old. Other change processes involve repeated or sequenced patterns, such as the repeated cycle of night and day or the steady growth of a seedling. Building with blocks or putting puzzles together involves changing shapes. Many kinds of change can be measured, such as a child's growth, the size of shadows at different times of day, or the temperature from morning to afternoon.

Some ideas to start you thinking about science:

> **Idea** The concept of change is central to science investigations. In physical science, children observe and predict how different objects, toys, equipment, and materials change in different situations. These situations include the following: applying energy (heat, light, sound) and force (pushing, pulling). Changes in living things over time is a big theme of life science. Earth and space science examines changes in the land and in the sky. And finally, a critical idea in technology is that, over time, inventions designed and made by people have changed the way we accomplish tasks.

Some ideas to start you thinking about language and literacy:

> **Idea** As children tune in to the idea of change, they will begin noticing some kind of change in nearly every book that is read to them. Characters change, buildings and places change, seasons change, and weather changes. Noticing the changes that take place in stories is a great way for children to build reading comprehension skills.

## VOCABULARY

**cycle:** an interval of time during which a characteristic or regularly repeated event or sequence occurs

**decompose:** cause something to decay or rot

**germinate:** when a seed begins to grow and put out shoots after a period of dormancy

**grow:** undergo natural or human-made development by increasing in size and changing physically

**habitat:** the natural home or environment of an animal, plant, or other organism

There are many books to explore with children about growing and changing. Here are a few suggestions:

*I'm Growing!* by Aliki

*You'll Soon Grow Into Them, Titch* by Pat Hutchins

*Arabella Miller's Tiny Caterpillar* by Clare Jarrett

*Jody's Beans* by Malachy Doyle

*How a Seed Grows* by Helene Jordan

*A Log's Life* by Wendy Pfeffer

*I Stink!* by Jim and Kate McMullan

# INVESTIGATION: WE CHANGE, TOO!

Children collect and examine pictures of themselves or other people of different ages. They match and sort pictures, notice changes, and sequence pictures from younger to older.

## WHAT'S NEEDED

collection of pictures of people of many different ages (This collection can be a mixture of photographs of the children in your group and pictures of children and adults of all ages from magazines and catalogs.)

**Note**: You'll also need long strips of paper, cardboard, or poster board for mounting pictures side-by-side and clear contact paper. This is optional, but since children will be handling this collection a lot, you may want to mount the pictures on cardboard or poster board and wrap the pictures with clear contact paper.

Read a book such as *Feast for 10* by Cathryn Falwell to explore the topic of growing and changing with the children.

## THINGS TO CONSIDER

○ You are apt to discover that some families have many photographs of their children while other families have very few. By creating one large collection that is a mixture of photographs sent in by families and pictures from magazines and catalogs, you can alleviate any hard feelings that children might experience. You can also print a photo of children who do not bring one in from home.

## KEY SCIENCE STANDARDS CHILDREN PRACTICE

**Life Science:** observing, naming, and discussing physical characteristics, basic needs, ways of moving, growth patterns, life cycles, and human interdependence

**Science as Inquiry:** estimating and predicting by imagining how people will change in the future

**Science as Inquiry:** noticing change over time by describing the differences between younger and older people

**Science as Inquiry:** recognizing relationships by comparing shapes, sizes, and features of different-aged people

**Science as Inquiry:** sorting and classifying by grouping pictures of people of similar ages

## STEP BY STEP

1. Work together building your collection of pictures. Ask families to send in photographs and help the children cut out pictures from magazines and catalogs.
2. Lay out the picture collection on a table or floor. Allow the children plenty of time to look at and talk about the various pictures.
3. Talk together about sorting the pictures. What sorting characteristics can the children think of? Some possibilities are:

- By age groups,
- By pairs of people about the same age, and
- By a sequence from youngest to oldest or oldest to youngest.

### Talk with Children

- Challenge the children to notice more details about the pictures each time they examine them:

  *Let's see if we can find something we've never observed before!*

- Talk about the similarities and differences among the different-aged people:

  *What's different about this baby and this toddler? What's the same?*

- Teach the children words for the different stages of human growth: *babies, toddlers, young children, teenagers, adults,* and so on.

- Ask the children to explain why they match, sort, or sequence as they do; record and display their explanations:

  *Tell me why you put those pictures together. I'll write your words to hang on the wall.*

### Observe Children

- How do the children match, sort, and sequence the pictures? (by size? by color of clothes? by randomly putting pictures together?)

- How do the children describe similarities, differences, and changes over time? (by using comparative size words, such as *bigger than, smaller than, older than, younger than*? by saying "Just because"? by simply stating, "They're the same," or "They're different"?)

- How do the children explain human growth and change? (with scientific explanations, such as "He ate his food" or "She took her vitamins"? with magical explanations, such as "It just happens," or "Mommy makes it happen"? with random explanations, such as "Because I get my hair cut"?)

## EXTEND THE LEARNING

- Make *Now I'm Growing!* books with children. Use drawings or photographs of children in your group to make a group book to display.

## CONNECT WITH FAMILIES

Display examples of your sorting and the following:

### We Change, Too!

To help us learn more about how humans grow and develop, we have been investigating a collection of photographs of people of all ages. We've been sorting these photographs by many different characteristics. As we did this sorting and talking we practiced:

- Using descriptive language about what we noticed,
- Talking about how all living things grow and change,
- Sorting by grouping pictures by different characteristics, and
- Recognizing similarities and differences.

# INVESTIGATION: HOW DOES IT CHANGE?

In our everyday lives we see natural changes through the seasons. We also see changes that are made by humans such as roads and houses. In this investigation, children begin to learn about changes they can make to objects.

## WHAT'S NEEDED

clear plastic cups
small sponges or cut-up pieces of sponges
sugar cubes

Read a book about changes such as *Changes, Changes* by Pat Hutchins when you do this investigation with the children.

## THINGS TO CONSIDER

○ You may want to give each child a cup or have them work together in small groups.

## KEY SCIENCE STANDARDS CHILDREN PRACTICE

**Physical Science:** observing and discussing the characteristics of various materials
**Science as Inquiry:** asking questions about the investigation
**Science as Inquiry:** noticing change over time by observing what happens to various objects when placed in water
**Science as Inquiry:** noticing similarities and differences
**Science as Inquiry:** predicting what will happen to the sponge and sugar cube

## STEP BY STEP

1. Gather a small group of children around a table. Hand out the sponge pieces first, keeping some aside for comparisons. Ask the children what they know about these dry pieces. Encourage them to use words that describe the sponges now, before they get wet.

2. Ask the children what they think will happen to the sponge pieces when they're put in water.

3. Bring out the cups and water. Have the children put the sponge pieces in the cups. Talk together about what is happening in the cups.

4. Sponges take up—absorb—water quickly, so the children can take them out of the water fairly soon and observe similarities and differences. Encourage discussion about what they have noticed.
   *What changed?*
   *What did not?*
   *Is there a way to figure out how much water a sponge piece took up—absorbed?*

5. Next, use sugar cubes instead of sponge pieces. What do the children know about these white cubes? What do they expect will happen to them in water?

6. Have the children put one cube in each cup. Observe what happens and discuss any changes that children notice.

MATH AND SCIENCE INVESTIGATIONS

7. Try putting cubes in two cups at the same time. Stir the water in one cup, while leaving the other one alone.

    *What is different or the same about the two cups?*

8. Plan to repeat this investigation in the future, testing the same materials again or other ones suggested by the children.

## Talk with Children

○ Encourage discussion of the changes children notice in the sponges and the changes they observe after they put in the sugar cubes. You might ask:

    *Did all the sponge pieces change in the same way?*

    *Did the water change at all?*

    *What happened to the sugar?*

○ If the children test other objects, remember to ask them to predict what they think will happen before testing a new object.

○ Be sure to introduce new vocabulary when the children are ready. The sugar cube *dissolves*. The sponge *absorbs* water.

## Observe Children

○ Children are fascinated by the ways in which things change. Some changes are almost magical to them, such as the sugar cube dissolving. Notice how they describe this change. Some children may say that the sugar cube melts while others may say that it disappears. Ask the children to describe where they think the sugar has gone when they cannot see it.

○ Record the descriptive words the children use to talk about changes that they notice.

○ Do they make connections to changes in other things that they have seen?

## EXTEND THE LEARNING

○ On walks with the children, begin to help them make the distinction between human-made changes and natural changes. Compare a piece of sidewalk cement with a rock: They have a lot in common, but their origin is different. Explain this to the children, and ask them about the differences between other kinds of natural and unnatural changes, such as:

    Ice formed by freezing on a pond and ice formed in the freezer,

    Air-conditioning and a cool breeze, or

    An open field and a flower garden.

## CONNECT WITH FAMILIES

Display the following:

### How Does It Change?

We've been experimenting with how objects change in water. Using sponges and sugar cubes, we predicted and then observed how these objects change in water. We also learned that water can change objects, but some objects are not changed by water. When we did this investigation we practiced:

• Observing change in a scientific experiment, and

• Predicting and changing our predictions.

Growing and Changing

# INVESTIGATION: WHAT'S INSIDE?

In this investigation children observe and compare the variety of seeds inside fruits.

## WHAT'S NEEDED
chart paper or poster board
cutting board
knife (for adult use only)
magnifying glasses
markers
paper plates or paper towels
selection of fruits and vegetables with seeds such as an apple, banana, and green pepper, and one or two fruits and vegetables without seeds such as a carrot, potato, and celery stalk

**Note**: If you're working with one group of children, you'll want to have at least four or five fruits/vegetables so that children will be able to make many predictions and explorations once the fruits and vegetables are cut open.

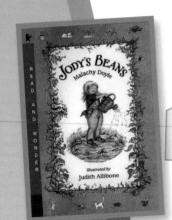

A book such as *Jody's Beans* by Malachy Doyle is an excellent way to introduce seeds and fruits to the children.

## THINGS TO CONSIDER
O  Ask families about children's food allergies as you plan this investigation.

The plant material we eat is divided into the categories of fruits and vegetables. Fruits are usually fleshy, often juicy and sweet. Vegetables can also be juicy and sweet, but are considered foods to put in a salad or have with lunch or dinner.

However, technically, if the plant part we eat has seeds, it's a fruit. That means that peppers, tomatoes, and so on are all fruits! The other parts of plants that we eat are leaves (lettuce, spinach) and stems (celery), roots or tubers (carrots, potatoes), and seeds (peas, beans).

## KEY MATH STANDARDS CHILDREN PRACTICE
**Numbers and Operations:** counting the seeds

## KEY SCIENCE STANDARDS CHILDREN PRACTICE
Life Science: exploring and talking about seeds
Science as Inquiry: asking scientific questions by naming and describing the food
Science as Inquiry: finding patterns by describing the seed patterns
Science as Inquiry: predicting how many seeds there will be and whether there will be any
Science as Inquiry: sorting and classifying by noticing the similarities and differences between and among the seed patterns

## STEP BY STEP

1. Place four or five fruits and vegetables on a table. Talk together about these items. Can children name them? What do the children know about how the fruits and vegetables taste? Have the children ever seen inside any of these foods? What is inside?

2. Make an illustrated chart with your group, drawing the fruits and vegetables along one side. In the next column, write the name of the fruit or vegetable.

3. Tell the children that some of these have seeds inside. Ask them to predict which will have the most seeds, which will have the least seeds, and which will have no seeds. Record the predictions in the next column (record all predictions).

4. After making and recording the predictions, cut open each of the items and look at the seed patterns. Allow the children time to observe the seeds with magnifying glasses. What do the children notice about the location and pattern of the seeds? Compare the seed patterns: Which are the same? Which are different?

5. Test your predictions by counting the seeds. Which has the most seeds? the least? none? Record your findings in the next column on your chart.

6. Talk about your chart. Which predictions were nearly accurate? Which ones were not even close? Talk about the new and interesting things you observed and explored.

## Talk with Children

○ Encourage the children to use as many science inquiry skills as possible in this investigation.

○ Point out to the children the different senses they can use to investigate fruits and vegetables.

○ Encourage the children to make predictions and then observe to see if their predictions were correct.

## Observe Children

○ How do the children respond when you ask them to sort the fruits and vegetables in different ways?

○ Children will have different styles of getting involved in this activity. Who is an observer? Who is an active participant?

○ Many children enjoy drawing pictures about their discoveries. How do these drawings differ from one child to another?

○ As the children label, predict, and describe, listen to their language. Do the children use the names of the fruits and vegetables or do they point to them when they are talking?

○ What different things do the children say when you ask them to predict what is inside the fruits and vegetables?

○ How do the children describe what they see on the insides of the fruits and vegetables?

## EXTEND THE LEARNING

○ The children can plant some of the seeds in cups of soil. They may be curious to see if a pumpkin seed or a cherry pit will sprout.

## CONNECT WITH FAMILIES

Display your chart along with the following:

### What's Inside?

We've been investigating the insides of different kinds of fruits and vegetables. We predicted what we expected to see and then checked our predictions. When we did this we practiced:

• Asking scientific questions such as What's that?, Why does it look that way?, What is that for?;

• Making predictions and checking them;

• Using a hand lens; and

• Talking about different parts of fruits and vegetables: seeds, rinds, and flesh.

# INVESTIGATION: SEED TO SEED

Children love to plant seeds and watch them sprout and grow. This investigation involves exploring the life of a plant, from seed germination to decomposition.

## WHAT'S NEEDED
Listed separately. Each part of this investigation requires different materials.

Read a book such as *Jody's Beans* by Malachy Doyle while you do this investigation with the children.

## THINGS TO CONSIDER
○ Do the children in your group have experience with seeds and/or growing plants?

## KEY MATH STANDARDS CHILDREN PRACTICE
**Communicating:** creating a growth chart
**Measuring:** recording the height of each seedling with yarn
**Representing:** graphing the height of each seedling

## KEY SCIENCE STANDARDS CHILDREN PRACTICE
**Life Science:** discovering and observing the various parts of a plant like the stem, leaves, and roots
**Life Science:** planting, watering, and watching a seedling grow
**Science as Inquiry:** asking scientific questions about seedlings
**Science as Inquiry:** noticing change over time
**Science as Inquiry:** observing a seed as it germinates
**Science as Inquiry:** predicting what will happen
**Science as Inquiry:** recording data

## EXTEND THE LEARNING: GERMINATING SEEDS

## WHAT'S NEEDED
assortment of seeds
magnifying glasses
paper plates
paper towels
water

## STEP BY STEP
1. Place an assortment of seeds between moist white paper towels held between two plates (to preserve the moisture).
2. Place a few seeds on a plate and keep these seeds dry for comparisons and discussion.

3. Check the seeds daily to make sure the towels are still damp. In five to seven days, most of the seeds will have germinated.

4. Using magnifying glasses, encourage the children to observe and discuss the ways the seeds have changed from their dry form. Ask:
   *How is this (germinated) seed different from the dry seed?*
   Some of the seeds will not have germinated. Ask:
   *Why do you think this happened?*

5. Discuss all the possible reasons (temperature, moisture, light, and so on) and introduce an experiment to discover one or more possible reasons.

## EXTEND LEARNING: WATCH IT GROW!

### WHAT'S NEEDED

bean seeds

graphs and/or a camera

**Note:** This is a great project for collecting data with photographs.

paper for drawing

pots or cups

potting soil

spoons for scooping soil

water

yarn or string for measuring

Read a book about how a seed grows, such as *Jody's Beans* by Malachy Doyle. Go back and look at and talk about the pictures.

### STEP BY STEP

1. Have the children work together filling five or six cups or pots with soil and plant two or three seeds below the soil's surface. Water the seeds well. Talk together about what seeds need to germinate and grow.

2. After germination, store the pots in a sunny spot for future observation. Add water when the soil gets dry. Continue the investigation by having the children observe the plants each day or week, depending on your program and the kind of bean seeds you used.

3. As the seeds sprout, talk about what you see.
   *What do you notice?*
   *How many leaves do you see?*

4. Measure the plants. On a large piece of paper, draw a line at the bottom representing the top level of the soil the plants are growing in.
   Tape each cut piece of yarn or string vertically, up from that line. Mark the date at the bottom of each measurement.

5. After a few weeks you will have a growth chart of the plants you have measured. Talk with the children about this visual chart of the plants' growth.

MATH AND SCIENCE INVESTIGATIONS

6. Have the children make drawings of the plants at their different growth stages. Help the children label their drawings with the correct scientific terms for plant parts.

Prompt children to talk about their observations:

*Tell me about your drawing.*

*What do you predict the plant will look like the next time you see it?*

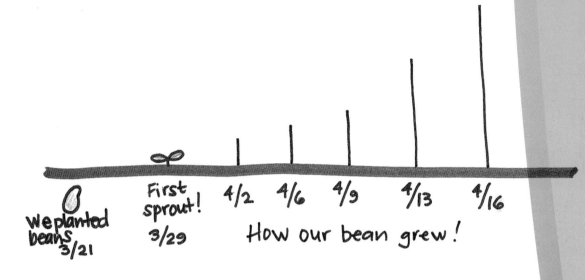

We planted beans 3/21

First sprout! 3/29

4/2   4/6   4/9   4/13   4/16

How our bean grew!

Most plants need air, water, light, and food to live and grow.

Most plants make seeds for new plants.

Plants closely resemble their parents.

Plants have *life cycles* that include being born, developing into adults, reproducing, and eventually dying and *decomposing*. Life cycles are different for different plants.

Many foods we eat are seeds.

A *habitat* is the local environment in which a specific organism or species lives (pond, forest, and so on).

The *environment* is the natural world in which people, plants, and animals live.

## Talk with Children

○ Ask the children to talk about what they think will happen to the seeds in the soil.

○ Talk about why the seeds need soil and what else seeds need to grow.

○ Talk about any changes children notice as the plants grow.

○ Ask the children to describe the changes they see in the seedlings:

*How have the seedlings grown?*

*What do you notice that you didn't notice before?*

*What is new or different about the seedlings?*

○ Talk with the children about measuring:

*How else could we measure how the seedlings are growing?*

*What other kinds of measuring have you seen or done?*

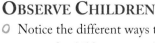

## OBSERVE CHILDREN

○ Notice the different ways the children show interest in this seed project. Which senses do children use as they work with the soil and the seeds? sight? smell? touch?

○ How accurate are the children's attempts to measure the plants with pieces of yarn?

○ How do different children stay involved in the seed investigation over time? by remembering to check the pots periodically? by drawing pictures at different stages? by talking about what they observe? by asking questions?

○ Listen to the children's explanations, questions, and descriptions. How do the children explain what seeds need in order to grow? What questions do the children ask? How do the children describe the changes they observe in the plants as they grow?

## EXTEND THE LEARNING: A SCIENTIFIC EXPERIMENT

## WHAT'S NEEDED

assortment of seeds
magnifying glasses
paper plates
paper towels
water

## STEP BY STEP

1. Repeat the paper towel procedure from earlier in the investigation (the control) and then set one or more of the following conditions (variables) where everything is identical except for each variable:

○ Seeds presoaked for 24 hours,

○ Covered plates placed in bright sunlight (warm),

○ Soil placed between the towels and among the seeds, and

○ Seeds placed in dry paper towels.
   Be sure to label each variable.

2. In one week's time observe seeds with magnifying glasses (hand lenses) and make comparisons between and among the different growing conditions.

3. Encourage the children to talk about what they see. Ask:
   *How many seeds germinated in each situation?*
   *What might be some of the reasons for the differences in germination?*
   *Which were the best growing conditions?*
   *Why? What do seeds need in order to germinate?*

4. Display books about growing, photographs of the experiments, and samples from your experiment.

## CONNECT WITH FAMILIES

Display the Seed to Seed investigation materials. Also display the children's drawings along with the following information:

### Seed to Seed

We are learning about growing seeds and the life cycle of a plant. We are doing this by soaking seeds, sprouting seeds, and observing the growth of seeds. We also learned about the parts of a plant: seed, root, stem, and leaf. When we did this investigation we practiced:

- Observing carefully and make drawings of what we saw, and
- Measuring and recording our measurements.

MATH AND SCIENCE INVESTIGATIONS

# CHAPTER 9

# Same and Different

Ms. Gonzales is helping Crystal put together a puzzle. Out of the blue, Crystal says, "You're just like my other teacher."

Ms. Gonzales knows Crystal's other teacher and knows that there is no physical resemblance between the two of them. So, she asks Crystal, "How are we the same?" Crystal says, "You help me do puzzles just like my other teacher."

Human beings have a natural instinct to impose order and organization on their world. One very basic way we do this is to put things together that belong together. In kitchens, the measuring cups and spoons are usually in the same drawer. In workshops, the nails are often separated from the screws. In bedrooms, underwear is in one drawer, shirts in another, and pants in yet another. Logical thinking and reasoning begin with noticing how things are the same and different.

For young children, figuring out how things are the same or different is not as simple as it is for older children and adults. Objects have many characteristics, or attributes. They have color, shape, size, and texture, just to name a few. Young children tend to focus on just one characteristic or attribute at a time. In the story above, Crystal focused only on two people's approach to helping her with puzzles!

Here is another example: There was a red crayon and a red marker on the table and the teacher asked Jonas, "Are these the same?"

He said, "No," and then pointed to the marker, saying "marker" and pointed to the crayon, saying "crayon." Jonas was focusing on the fact that they were different kinds of objects, rather than on their shared color. In his eyes and mind, the two objects were very different. If the teacher had asked, "Are these the same color?," he would probably have said "Yes" because his attention had been drawn to the attribute or characteristic of color.

Initially, children look for similarities and differences and sort objects into groups that share one characteristic or attribute. Gradually, they begin to think more flexibly. They notice that things may be the same or different in more than one way. Anna had reached this stage:

Anna sat on the floor with a shoebox full of unpainted wooden shapes. There were three different shapes—circles, squares, and triangles. There were two different sizes of shapes—small and large. At first, she began sorting them by shape. Then she sorted each shape into groups of large and small. In the end, she had six sets: large and small circles, large and small squares, and large and small triangles.

Consider one more example:

While cleaning up his room, Michael lined up his stuffed animals on the bed, with the smallest one at the foot of the bed and the largest one at the head of the bed.

Michael is noticing how his animals are all different. Rather than grouping them by similarities, he separated them by size and put them in order.

**Some ideas to start you thinking about math:**

**Idea** Being able to notice similarities and differences helps children to begin logical thinking, reasoning, and problem solving. Two very important mathematical processes are problem solving and reasoning; both require logical thinking. Logical thinking involves moving from one step to the next in a way that makes sense.

Some ideas to start you thinking about science:

**Idea** "Science is a way of trying to discover the nature of things" (Karen Lind, *Exploring Science in Early Childhood Education*, Wadsworth Publishing, 1994, p. 53). These discoveries, however, are rarely accidental or lucky. They are usually the result of a well-thought-out, organized, step-by-step series of experiments. For young scientists, an important way to discover the "nature of things" is to notice the ways in which things are the same and different.

Some ideas to start you thinking about language and literacy:

**Idea** When children hear books read to them, one of the important ways they come to really understand or comprehend the story is to see similarities to and differences from their own lives and experiences. Some excellent questions to ask children about stories might be:
*How is this character the same as you?*
*How is this (house, place, story, family) the same or different from yours?*

## VOCABULARY

**attribute:** a recognizable characteristic of someone or something
**characteristic:** a feature or quality belonging to a person, place, or thing
**compare:** to describe something as similar to something else
**different:** unlike in form, quality, amount, or nature
**heavy:** of great weight
**light:** of little weight
**same:** identical or similar
**set:** a group of objects with one or more common attributes
**sorting loops:** a flexible border for enclosing sorted items. Loops allow groups to overlap when a shared attribute is seen in two distinct sets. Shoelaces work well.

Any books about collections or sorting are a great way to explore this topic with children. Here are a few suggestions:
*Five Creatures* by Emily Jenkins
*Hannah's Collections* by Marthe Jocelyn
*Bein' with You This Way* by W. Nikola-Lisa
*The Button Box* by Margarette S. Reid
*If You Find a Rock* by Peggy Christian
*Seashells by the Seashore* by Marianne Collins Berkes
*Zoe's Hats* by Sharon Lane Holm
*Just a Little Bit* by Ann Tompert

# INVESTIGATION: MYSTERY OBJECTS (I SPY)

Children touch an object and give clues about its characteristics (attributes): the size, shape, position, color, and so on.

## WHAT'S NEEDED

bag or box in which to hide the object
collection of small common objects: a toy car, a doll, a kitchen spoon, a straw, a block of wood, a piece of fruit

Read a book such as *Seven Blind Mice* by Ed Young as you do this investigation with the children.

## THINGS TO CONSIDER

○ Children will need good observation skills, good descriptive words, and time to take turns giving clues and guessing. The most important part of this activity is giving good clues. Help the children come up with clues that describe shape, color, and other attributes (characteristics). Remind them not to say the name of the object.

○ The guessers should not see the Mystery Object being placed in the bag or box.

○ This investigation can be repeated many, many times.

## KEY MATH STANDARDS CHILDREN PRACTICE

**Communicating:** using size and shape words to describe the mystery object

## KEY SCIENCE STANDARDS CHILDREN PRACTICE

**Physical Science:** describing properties of objects
**Science as Inquiry:** communicating information and ideas by describing how objects feel
**Science as Inquiry:** predicting by using clues to make informed guesses

## STEP BY STEP

1. Choose an object (an orange, for example) from the collection and put it in the bag or box.
2. Have one child reach into the bag or box, touch the object, and describe what he or she feels. The child might say:
   *It feels round. It must be a ball.*
3. Respond to the child's description by saying something like:
   *Yes, it's round, but it's not a ball.*
4. Ask another child to touch the object and describe what he or she feels. The child might say:
   *It's round, and it feels bumpy all over. It's a rock.*

MATH AND SCIENCE INVESTIGATIONS

5. Continue this process until a child figures out what the object is. Be sure to repeat the descriptions as each child touches the object. You may want to give additional clues such as (if the object is an orange, for example):
*You can make juice from it. It's a fruit.*

6. Take turns so that all the children have a chance to touch and describe an object.

## Talk with Children

○ Help the children use words that describe shape, texture, color, and other characteristics. Encourage the children to use a wide variety of descriptive words. For example, when talking about how an object feels, help them with words like *prickly, soft, smooth, hard, sharp, rounded,* or other words to describe texture and shape.

○ Use this opportunity to teach vocabulary. For example: Sara said it was bumpy and rough. Can anyone describe what *rough* means? Give the children plenty of time to talk about the words and their definitions.

## Observe Children

○ Listen to the children's language as they describe objects. Do they use the same words over and over, or do they use a variety of words to describe how things feel?

○ How do different children work in a group? Do some children discuss their ideas before making guesses? Are some children supportive of other children's comments?

## EXTEND THE LEARNING

○ Give each child an opportunity to select an object, put it in the bag or box, and repeat the descriptions.

## CONNECT WITH FAMILIES

Post the following:

### Mystery Objects

We've been using our senses to investigate "Mystery Objects." We hid an object in a bag and then used our hands to feel the object. As we did this investigation we practiced:

• Describing the properties of objects, and

• Predicting by using informed guesses or clues.

# INVESTIGATION: SINK AND FLOAT

Children experiment with objects that may either sink or float. They also make predictions, make observations, and sort the objects into groups.

## WHAT'S NEEDED
chart paper or poster board
markers
plastic tubs of water
sink-and-float collection—small objects that can get wet and not be ruined. Select heavy objects, light objects, objects that are made of different materials such as plastic, wood, and Styrofoam.
smocks or extra shirt (optional, but recommended)
sponges or soft cloths for cleanup

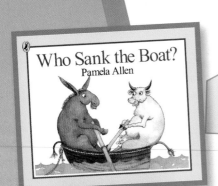

Read books such as *Mr. Gumpy's Outing* by John Burningham or *Who Sank the Boat?* by Pamela Allen as you do this investigation with the children.

## THINGS TO CONSIDER
O Group children three or four to a tub. It might be helpful for the children to wear smocks or to have an extra shirt available.
O After you're finished with this investigation, spread the objects out to allow them to dry.

## KEY MATH STANDARDS CHILDREN PRACTICE
**Data Analysis and Probability:** making a chart to show sinkers and floaters

## KEY SCIENCE STANDARDS CHILDREN PRACTICE
**Physical Science:** experimenting with water
**Science as Inquiry:** experimenting to see if objects sink or float
**Science as Inquiry:** observing to see what sinkers and floaters have in common
**Science as Inquiry:** predicting whether a given object will sink or float
**Science as Inquiry:** sorting objects into groups of sinkers and floaters

## STEP BY STEP
1. Allow the children time to explore the objects. Ask the children to put the objects in the water, one by one. Let them experiment and talk among themselves as you observe them.
2. Once the children have had time to experiment with sinking and floating, give them two sorting loops and ask them to sort the collection into sinkers and floaters. Are there some objects that both sink and float? Create a category for those objects as well.

MATH AND SCIENCE INVESTIGATIONS

3. After the children have experimented with sinking and floating, introduce more objects and challenge the children to make predictions and test their predictions.
4. Do this investigation several times over a period of days or weeks. Each time, add new and different objects to the sink-and-float collection.

| ITEM | PREDICTION | | WHAT HAPPENED | |
|---|---|---|---|---|
| | **SINK?** | **FLOAT?** | **SINK?** | **FLOAT?** |
| | | X | | X |
| | X | | | X |
| | X | | X | |
| | | X | X | |
| | | X | | X |
| | X | | X | |
| | | X | | X |
| | | X | X | |

## Talk with Children

○ As the children experiment with the objects, ask questions such as:
  *What do you notice about the ones that sink? What do you notice about the ones that float?*
  *What is the same about the sinkers? What is different about the floaters?*
  *What is the same about the floaters? What is different about the sinkers?*

○ As the children make predictions, ask them:
  *Why do you think this object will sink?*
  *Why do you think this object will float?*

○ Encourage the children to make comparisons between and among objects. Challenge the children with questions such as these:
  *Can you make a floater sink?*
  *Can you make a sinker float?*

## Observe Children

○ Notice how the children approach making predictions.
○ Listen to the children as they experiment. Do they compare objects to each other?
  *(That piece of wood floated, so I think this ruler will float, too.)*

○ How do they respond when you ask questions such as, "Why do you think some things float and others sink?" Do they look at and feel an object before predicting whether it will sink or float? Look for ways the children make connections to previous experiences.

### EXTEND THE LEARNING

○ Chart this investigation. Use a piece of chart paper or bulletin board to make a "Sinkers and Floaters" chart. One way to record this work is to have the children make charts with pictures of the objects that either sink or float.

### CONNECT WITH FAMILIES

○ Display photographs of the investigation and lists of objects that float or sink.

○ Post the following on a bulletin board:

> ## Sink and Float
>
> We've been investigating sinking and floating by putting objects in water. When we did this investigation, we practiced:
>
> • Making predictions and testing those predictions, and
>
> • Sorting a collection of objects based on an observed characteristic (sinking or floating).

MATH AND SCIENCE INVESTIGATIONS

# INVESTIGATION: SORTING A COLLECTION

Children explore similarities and differences by sorting a collection of objects.

## WHAT'S NEEDED

small containers for sorting collections

string or yarn to make sorting loops

variety of collections—buttons or rocks or shells or toys or dried beans

> Read a book such as *Hannah's Collections* by Marthe Jocelyn as you do this investigation with the children.

## THINGS TO CONSIDER

○ Children need plenty of time to freely explore the collections before using them in a structured way. Observing the children as they explore will help you know when they are ready for more complicated sorting activities.

○ Consider the age of the children when deciding what and how many collections to make available. For younger children, begin with collections that have less variety and complexity.

## KEY MATH STANDARDS CHILDREN PRACTICE

**Making Connections:** using sorting in everyday life, such as clean-up time

**Problem Solving:** using sorting as a way to organize materials

**Reasoning and Proof:** explaining why they sorted objects as they did

## KEY SCIENCE STANDARDS CHILDREN PRACTICE

**Physical Science:** identifying the physical properties of objects (size, shape, color, texture, weight, material, and so on)

**Science as Inquiry:** recognizing relationships by comparing objects (larger than, smaller than, more than, less than, and so on)

**Science as Inquiry:** sorting and classifying by noticing similarities and differences and putting objects into groups based on shared attributes

## STEP BY STEP

1. Put one of your collections (such as a button collection) out for the children to explore.

2. Talk with the children about the words *same* and *different*. Together, find things that are the same among the buttons. The children might suggest color, shape, or size.

3. Talk with the children about the word *attribute*. Use one of the attributes suggested by the children to start sorting the buttons. Attributes can be any characteristics, such as color, size, shape, or type of material. For example, ask the children to help you find all the red buttons.

4. Put a sorting loop (a circle of string or yarn) around the set the children have made, and tell them that this shows that these red buttons are a set because they all have the same attribute (the same color).

5. Have the children choose another attribute (such as square) and make another set. Place a sorting loop around this set of buttons. Again, show the children that the loop shows these buttons are a set. Ask them to notice and describe what is alike about the buttons.

6. Allow the children plenty of time to practice sorting buttons based on attributes. Ask the children to describe how they are sorting as they group buttons together.

7. Try this investigation again, using other collections such as rocks, shells, or small toys.

## Talk with Children

○ Validate the children's ideas:
*You noticed that some buttons have two holes and some have four—let's sort that way! George said that some of the cars were blue. Blue is a color, so let's sort these cars by that attribute.*

○ Guide the children's observations:
*What do you notice about the shapes of the blocks?*
*What makes some shapes the same?*
*What makes them different?*

○ Avoid solving problems for the children. Instead, get their ideas for solutions:
*Which sorting loop should this one go in? It has some red and some yellow on it. What should we do?*

○ Model the language of science: Use the words *attribute* and *set* as the children sort objects. The more children hear these words, the better they'll understand the concept and begin using the words themselves. You might say:
*This block is red, so I would sort it into the set of red objects.*
*Good work! You sorted those cars! Can you think of another attribute to sort by?*

○ Encourage the children to explain what they are doing as they sort:
*Why did you put that shell in that sorting loop?*

## Observe Children

○ What do the children do with the collections during free play? (sort? count? line up the objects? use for pretend play?)

○ How do the children decide how to sort objects? (copy others? use ideas from *Hannah's Collections*? invent original ideas?)

○ What do the children do when they finish sorting a collection one way? (put the collection away and get another? sort the collection another way? sort the collection again in the same way?)

○ What words do the children use as they sort? (*sort? attribute?* color, size, shape words? *all of these are...?*)

## EXTEND THE LEARNING

○ Set up a sorting area to encourage the children to sort on their own. Tape sorting loops in place or use colored tape. Change the materials periodically to keep interest high and to promote sorting by different attributes.

○ Provide the children with paper and crayons, pencils, or markers so that they can represent their sorting work.

○ Introduce the children to Venn diagrams. A Venn diagram is a way to represent two sets of objects that have both individual attributes and a shared attribute. For example, if buttons are being sorted by the colors black and white, the two loops would overlap, creating a third space for the buttons that are both black and white.

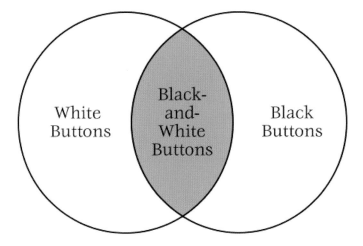

## CONNECT WITH FAMILIES

Post the following on a bulletin board:

### Sorting a Collection

We have been sorting collections of different objects according to their attributes. Using sorting loops, we sorted according to shape, size, color, or texture. When we sorted and used sorting loops, we practiced:

• Using vocabulary to describe the different characteristics of objects,

• Using observation skills to notice differences, and

• Using classification skills to group similar objects together.

# INVESTIGATION: WHAT'S THE RULE?

Children explore ways to sort all kinds of objects and then take turns guessing each other's sorting rules. As one child sorts silently, the others try to guess the sorting rule being used.

## WHAT'S NEEDED

sorting collection containing objects such as a shell, shape block, clothespin, paper clip, button, old key, jar and bottle lid or cap, small toy car or truck, stuffed animal, doll or action figure, and a plastic fruit or vegetable

string or yarn to make sorting loops

**Note**: Try to find objects of different colors, shapes, sizes, textures, appearances (shiny or dull), and functions. Use your imagination—the possibilities are endless.

Reading books such as *Bein' with You This Way* by W. Nikola-Lisa or *Five Creatures* by Emily Jenkins are excellent ways to introduce sorting and attributes to the children.

## THINGS TO CONSIDER

○ Because you will do this investigation with children who have some experience with collections and sorting, the children may be able to gather most of the materials themselves.

## KEY MATH STANDARDS CHILDREN PRACTICE

**Making Connections:** using sorting in everyday life, such as clean-up time

**Problem Solving:** using sorting as a way to organize materials

**Reasoning and Proof:** explaining why they sorted objects as they did

## KEY SCIENCE STANDARDS CHILDREN PRACTICE

**Physical Science:** identifying the physical properties of objects (size, shape, color, texture, weight, material, and so on)

**Science as Inquiry:** recognizing relationships by comparing objects (larger than, smaller than, more than, less than, and so on)

**Science as Inquiry:** sorting and classifying by noticing similarities and differences and putting objects into groups based on shared attributes

## STEP BY STEP

1. Let the children explore the collected objects. Give them lots of time to look at, touch, and talk about the objects.
2. Show the children how to do this investigation by modeling a "What's My Rule?" sort. Choose an attribute to sort by. For example, find all the shiny things. Or, you might choose all the objects made of wood, or all the objects you might use in the kitchen.

3. After you've placed the objects you selected in a sorting loop, ask the children:

   *What was my sorting rule?*

   Allow the children plenty of time to try to figure out your rule. You may want to model this sorting investigation many times.

4. Have the children take turns being the "sorter."

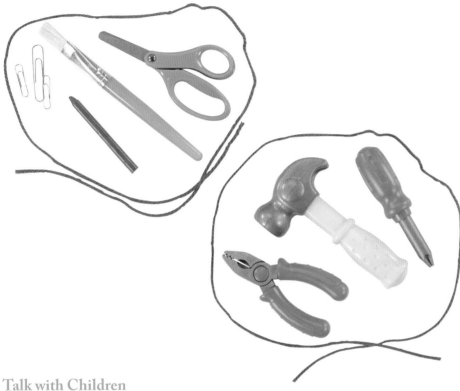

## Talk with Children

○ Encourage creative sorting rules:

*Wow! I don't think I would have thought of using the textures as a sorting rule. What a creative idea!*

○ Guide the children's observations to help them guess the rule:

*What do you notice about all the objects in this sorting loop?*

*How are they different from the ones in that sorting loop?*

*What could be the rule?*

*Is it about their color?*

*Is it about how you use the objects?*

○ Introduce science vocabulary during this investigation: Use a variety of words to describe the size, shape, color, and texture of the objects.

## Observe Children

○ Do some children prefer to be the sorter rather than the guesser? Do some prefer to be the guesser rather than the sorter?

○ Are there some children who enjoy coming up with tricky rules that are really hard to guess? What are those tricky rules?

○ How do the children express their sorting rule? (*I sorted by color. These are all square. These are the same and those are different.*)

## EXTEND THE LEARNING

○ Challenge the children to sort by two attributes for example: Things that are blue and shiny. Things that are circles and have red on them.

○ Leave sorting collections out so that the children can sort and re-sort as often as they choose.

## CONNECT WITH FAMILIES

○ Include a list of the different sorting rules used by the children. Challenge families to sort the collections and come up with their own rules.

○ Post the following on a bulletin board:

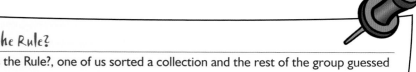

### What's the Rule?

In What's the Rule?, one of us sorted a collection and the rest of the group guessed what rule was used for sorting. By doing this investigation, we practiced:

• Sorting objects by different physical characteristics such as wooden, shiny, metallic, solid, flexible, dull, translucent, and opaque, and

• Investigating the concepts of *same* and *different*, and we learned that things can be the same in one way but different in other ways.

# INVESTIGATION: SORTING ANIMALS

Children describe and sort pictures of animals by many different characteristics.

## WHAT'S NEEDED
collection of pictures of many different animals
construction paper, chart paper, or poster board
markers
string or yarn to make sorting loops

Read a book such as *Five Creatures* by Emily Jenkins as you do this investigation with the children.

## THINGS TO CONSIDER
○ Review your notes about other sorting investigations you and the children have worked on.

## KEY MATH STANDARDS CHILDREN PRACTICE
**Making Connections:** using sorting in everyday life, such as clean-up time
**Problem Solving:** using sorting as a way to organize animals
**Reasoning and Proof:** explaining why they sorted as they did

## KEY SCIENCE STANDARDS CHILDREN PRACTICE
**Life Science:** observing and talking about physical characteristics such as basic needs, habitats, ways of moving, appearances
**Science as Inquiry:** recognizing relationships: comparing animal characteristics
**Science as Inquiry:** sorting and classifying: noticing similarities and differences and putting animals into groups based on shared attributes

## STEP BY STEP
1. Talk with the children about the other sorting investigations they've done. What do they remember about sorting? Help the children remember the meaning of words like *characteristic* and *attribute*. Do they remember how to use the sorting loops? Can anyone make a sorting loop?
2. Allow plenty of time to look at and talk about the animal pictures.
   *What do you notice about sizes? Colors? Numbers of legs?*
   *What else do you know about the various animals? What do they eat? How do they move? Where do they live?*
   Make a sign with words or drawings depicting the different attributes: Animals with Wings, Animals on the Farm, Animals with Four Legs, Animals in the Water, and so on. Encourage the children to identify the names of these attributes. Remember: There is no right or wrong name for a group as long as all the children agree on the grouping attribute.

3. Ask the children to begin sorting the collection. Let the children take turns choosing an animal and explaining why that animal belongs to a specific group. As the children sort they may find attributes for which you have no group with a sign—make another attribute sign.

## Talk with Children

O Some children may have to count the number of legs before putting the animal into a group. Encourage this.

O When a child puts an animal into the wrong attribute group, ask the other children to help find the right group by describing what the sorting attribute is.

## Observe Children

O Notice how the children decide which animal goes in what group. Do they just look at it and put it in the correct group? Do they study the animal carefully? Do they ask other children for help?

O Listen for how the children describe the animals. Do they have a lot of information about different animals? Do they use descriptive words about how the animal looks or moves?

## EXTEND THE LEARNING

O Gather a collection of tools that could include drawing tools such as a pencil, paintbrush, or marker as well as kitchen tools, sewing tools, personal hygiene tools, or woodworking tools. Allow the children plenty of time to sort the tools by similar characteristics such as tools used for writing, for cooking, for cutting, for cleaning, to make a building, to make a dress, tools for measuring or mixing, and so on. Or sort the tools by which ones have numbers on them (measuring cups and a tape measure, for example), or group them by the shapes they have (the saw has a rectangle, the spoon has an oval).

## CONNECT WITH FAMILIES

O Display the animal pictures you sorted, along with a list of the many ways you sorted.

O Post the following on your bulletin board:

### Sorting Animals

We sorted pictures of animals many different ways. We learned that one animal can be in two different groups at the same time and we also learned about many physical characteristics of different animals. By sorting a collection of animals, we practiced comparing similarities and differences among animals.

# INVESTIGATION: HEAVY AND LIGHT

Children explore the concepts of *heavy* and *light* by holding various objects in their hands.

## WHAT'S NEEDED

collection of six or eight objects of various weights, such as a can of soup, a pencil, a tissue, a bar of soap, a stick of gum, and a book

magazine

markers

paper

scissors

tape or glue

Read a book such as *Just a Little Bit* by Ann Tompert with the children as you do this investigation.

## THINGS TO CONSIDER

○ Explain that when the object in your hand is heavy, your hand goes down, and when the object is light, your hand will go up.

○ Make sure that the two objects being compared differ greatly in weight.

○ The purpose of this investigation is to help children understand that *heavy* and *light* are meaningful terms only when making comparisons. In other words, one object is light only when it is compared to an object that is heavier.

○ Be sure to use the word *compare* during the investigation. Remind the children that when we use words like *heavy* and *light*, we are making a comparison.

## KEY MATH STANDARDS CHILDREN PRACTICE

Measuring: understanding and using comparative measurement words by describing objects as *heavier than*, *lighter than*, or *the same as*

## KEY SCIENCE STANDARDS CHILDREN PRACTICE

Physical Science: learning about weight as a physical property

Science as Inquiry: estimating and predicting when comparing objects

Science as Inquiry: recognizing relationships when comparing relative weights

## STEP BY STEP

1. Talk about *heavy* and *light* with the children. Ask:

   *If you had an elephant in one hand, and a mouse in the other, where would your hands be?*

   Allow each child to show where an elephant would be and where a mouse would be. Tell the children that when they do this, their arms are just like a seesaw.

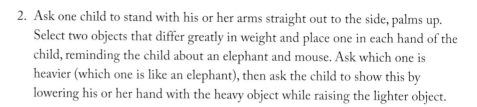

2. Ask one child to stand with his or her arms straight out to the side, palms up. Select two objects that differ greatly in weight and place one in each hand of the child, reminding the child about an elephant and mouse. Ask which one is heavier (which one is like an elephant), then ask the child to show this by lowering his or her hand with the heavy object while raising the lighter object.

Have the children take turns being the human balance with "heavy" arms going lower and "light" arms going up.

3. After each child has lots of practice, allow the children to choose their own two objects and to make a comparison sentence, such as:
   *The book is heavier than the pen.*
   *The pen is lighter than the book.*
   *The paper clip is the same as the pen.*

Do this investigation many times so that all the children have the opportunity to understand the concepts of *heavy* and *light*.

## Talk with Children

○ Model language: Ask the children to compare the two objects. Which is heavier? Which is lighter?
○ Clarify what the children tell you, using math and science vocabulary:
   *Are you saying that the toy phone weighs more than the feather? So the feather is lighter than the phone?*

## Observe Children

○ Do some children prefer to watch before trying?
○ Can the children recognize different weights of objects and lower the hand holding the heavier object?
○ What do the children do when the objects in each hand are close to the same weight?
○ Listen to the words the children use during this activity. Which children are using the words *heavy, light, heavier than, lighter than*?
○ Are the children making predictions? *This one will be heavier. This one will be lighter.*

## EXTEND THE LEARNING

○ Make a group *Heavy and Light Big Book*. Have each child either draw a picture of an object or cut a picture out of a magazine. Display all the pictures on a table and allow the children to make comparisons. Find pairs of heavy and light objects and put the book together, using these pairs. Write the book together. For example, a left-hand page might have a picture of something heavy and the words will say, "A rock is heavier..." The right-hand page would have a picture of something light and the words will say, "than a feather." The next page could show a bulldozer and say, "A bulldozer is heavier..." and the next page would say "than a rock."

## CONNECT WITH FAMILIES

Display the items you used in this investigation along with the following:

### Heavy and Light

We've been learning about heavy and light. We used these objects to make comparisons about heavy and light. We made our arms go down with heavy objects and up with light objects. When we did this investigation we practiced:

• Using comparative words such as *heavier than* and *lighter than* and

• Estimating and predicting when comparing objects.

# INVESTIGATION: EXPLORING A BALANCE

Children explore a balance by placing a variety of objects in the containers of a balance.

## WHAT'S NEEDED

collection of pennies or other nonstandard weights
collection of small objects of various weights
pan balance scale

## THINGS TO CONSIDER

O You'll want to give children plenty of opportunities to use the balance.

O The balance works best if it's set up on top of a large book, blocks, or box on a table so that the containers can move up or down freely.

## KEY MATH STANDARDS CHILDREN PRACTICE

**Measuring:** using comparative measurement words such as *heavier than* and *lighter than*, and estimating weight of objects
**Numbers and Operations:** counting objects
**Problem Solving:** using guessing and checking to test predictions

## KEY SCIENCE STANDARDS CHILDREN PRACTICE

**Physical Science:** learning about weight as a physical property
**Science as Inquiry:** experimenting by using the balance to answer questions
**Science as Inquiry:** measuring with nonstandard weights
**Science as Inquiry:** using simple tools when using the balance

## STEP BY STEP

1. Look carefully at each picture in a book such as *Just a Little Bit* by Ann Tompert and talk with the children about what is happening in the story. *Just a Little Bit* is a story about an elephant and a mouse. You might say:
   *Elephant is so heavy that it takes many other animals to balance the seesaw. The two sides of the seesaw have to be balanced for it to work.*

2. Introduce the children to the balance, explaining that a balance is a tool for weighing things. Show them how the balance works just like a seesaw. Show the children how to adjust the empty balance so that the containers are level.

3. Working with one child at a time, ask the child to put a heavy object in one of the balance containers. Then ask the child to find another object or objects that will balance the other. Encourage the child to keep experimenting until the balance containers are even. You might say:
   *When you put an object on one side of the balance, what do you have to add to the other side to make it balance?*

4. Encourage a few children at a time to experiment with the balance and objects. You can present challenges:

O Show the children two objects and ask them to predict which is heavier. Use the balance to test their predictions.

O Can the children find the heaviest and the lightest object in the collection?

- Ask the children to find out how many pennies (or other nonstandard weights that you may have available) will balance a toy tiger or any other object of interest to children.
- Challenge older children to put three objects in order from lightest to heaviest by comparing them using the balance. This might be a real challenge!

## Talk with Children

- As the children experiment with the balance, ask questions such as:
  *What happens when you put a heavy object in one side of the balance?*
  *How is this like the elephant on the seesaw?*
  *What can you do to make the two sides balance?*
- Once the children have had an opportunity to use the balance, encourage them to use language to compare the objects by using terms such as *heavier than*, *lighter than*, and *the same as*.

## Observe Children

- Notice how children use the balance differently to solve problems and test ideas.
  *Do they wait after adding an item to the balance to see what happens?*
  *What do they do to try to make the balance equal?*
- Listen to the children's words and ideas as they use the balance.
  *Are some children beginning to use the word* balance *as they experiment?*
- What do the children talk about as they add or take away objects from the balance?
  *Do they make comparisons of objects?*
  *Do they make predictions?*
  *Do they use the terms* heavier than *or* lighter than?

## EXTEND THE LEARNING

- Encourage the children to use the balance to predict and experiment using a variety of materials. Keep your "balancing collection" in a box or bag near the balance. For example, encourage the children to use it in the building, cooking, housekeeping, or sand table area.

## CONNECT WITH FAMILIES

- Display the balance along with the collection of objects used with the balance.
- Post the following on a bulletin board:

Exploring a Balance

We've been learning to use a simple balance, predicting and comparing what different objects weigh. When we used the balance we practiced:

- Putting items in order from lightest to heaviest or heaviest to lightest,
- Using nonstandard weights (pennies, paper clips, or pebbles) to compare different objects, and
- Counting carefully as we weighed items.

# CHAPTER 10
# Making It Work

In everyday life, we confront problems that need solving, dilemmas that need resolving, challenges that need conquering, puzzles that need untangling, quandaries that need clarifying, and questions that need responses. When children tackle building projects, they are also challenging themselves to "make it work."

Making It Work is about learning math, science, and literacy skills that help us work through predicaments with creativity, imagination, and inventiveness.

Children are intrigued with problems, challenges, puzzles, quandaries, and questions. They bring a supply of creativity, imagination, and inventiveness to these situations.

As you read the following quotes from children, you can almost hear their brains working as they come up with solutions, answers, and discoveries:

What will we do when the puppy grows bigger and won't fit into this little bed any more?

I'm five and you're four. That means I'm older than you.

I wanted to build a boat with my blocks, but the table wasn't big enough, so I decided to build on the floor.

I want to make the tallest tower, but I have to figure out which block shape will make my tower stronger.

We have only one apple, so we'll have to cut it into three pieces.

Children's natural inclination to conquer challenges, solve puzzles, and explain the unexplainable can be encouraged by using some simple strategies. Consider these examples:

Let children solve problems:
*Hmmm, can you figure out how to fit those tools into the box?*
Help children think about what they need to solve problems:
*What else do you need to help you finish building your fort?*
Encourage children to think of multiple approaches to a problem:
*What else could you try?*
Ask children to talk about their problem-solving strategies:
*How did you figure out that we needed three more cookies?*
Make children feel successful:
*You worked very hard to solve that problem. You must feel great!*

In addition, research shows that children's block play is related to later math competence. Block play provides a natural context for exploring the natural world. Like scientists, children can experiment with structures and observe outcomes of their building efforts. Through this process they learn about mass, weight, proportionality, and balance and can use their new concepts to plan and predict outcomes.

Shaklee, H. and Demarest, D. 2006. *Blockfest, Math and science learning for young children and their parents.* Boise, ID: University of Idaho Extension Parents as Teachers. August.

**Some ideas to start you thinking about math:**

**Idea** In the past, learning mathematics focused on memorizing number facts, shape names, how many inches in a foot, algebraic formulas, and so on. Today, the emphasis in mathematics is on using mathematical information to think through a great variety of problems. In addition to math knowledge, working on problems requires persistence to keep trying, flexibility to think of more than one strategy, creativity to invent unique approaches to problems, and confidence to trust one's own ideas.

**Some ideas to start you thinking about science:**

**Idea** When we think about science as a process of observing, posing questions, and pursuing answers to those questions, it is easy to see the link to problem solving. The inquiry skills of science all begin with curiosity. The basic instinct to wonder, ask questions, pursue answers, and make it work is the foundation for conducting experiments, gathering data, and explaining conclusions.

**Some ideas to start you thinking about language and literacy:**

**Idea** Communication is cited in both the math and science standards as a critical skill because talking and listening to one another is such a powerful way to learn and think. Language and vocabulary development occur as children explain how they solve problems and listen to the explanations of others. Because conversations motivate people to share ideas with each other, they offer children the opportunity to practice new words and new ways of expressing their ideas.

## VOCABULARY

**enclose:** to surround something or shut something in

**gravity:** the mutual force of attraction between all bodies that have mass

**ingenuity:** cleverness and originality

**problem:** a difficult situation that requires a solution

**stable:** steady or firm and not liable to move

Look for books about building or inventions. Here are a few suggestions:
*Lottie's New Beach Towel* by Petra Mathers
*Who Sank the Boat?* by Pamela Allen
*Albert's Alphabet* by Leslie Tryon
*Let's try it Out with Towers and Bridges* by Seymour Simon
*The Three Little Pigs* by Paul Galdone
*The Three Little Javelinas* by Susan Lowell
*Changes, Changes* by Pat Hutchins

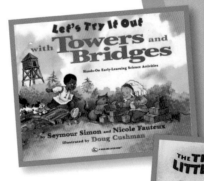

# INVESTIGATION: WHAT WOULD YOU DO IF...?

In this investigation children, brainstorm and playact different ways to solve a problem.

## WHAT'S NEEDED

beach towels or something to represent beach towels—perhaps a blanket or a large piece of cloth
everyday objects, such as wooden spoons, a jump rope, blocks, a box
markers
paper

*Lottie's New Beach Towel* by Petra Mathers is a great book to read with the children as you do this investigation.

## THINGS TO CONSIDER

○ This investigation is lively. Think of ways to refocus active children.
○ The children will need a large space in which to playact their solutions.

## KEY MATH STANDARDS CHILDREN PRACTICE

**Data Analysis:** collecting data to answer simple questions including the materials used and the solutions

## KEY SCIENCE STANDARDS CHILDREN PRACTICE

**Design Technology:** noticing a problem and suggesting solutions
**Design Technology:** responding to "what if...?" questions
**Science as Inquiry:** asking scientific questions such as "What would you do if...?"
**Science as Inquiry:** communicating information and ideas

## STEP BY STEP

1. Talk with the children about this problem: a boy wants to get from the ocean to his blanket but the sand is too hot to walk on.
2. Talk about problems and solutions. Remind the children that a problem can have more than one solution.
3. Engage the children in a conversation about the boy's problem (getting across the hot sand) and how he might solve it. Suggest one way he might solve his problem.
4. Show the children your "beach towel." Brainstorm with the children ways they might use the beach towel to get across hot sand. Have the children act out their solutions.
5. Let the children examine and talk about your collection of materials. Encourage them to use the different materials—rope, spoon, box, and other objects to solve the problem of getting across the hot sand. Have the children talk about and act out their solutions.

6. Collect your data: Make a chart of materials (towels, rope, spoon, box, and so on) and ask the children to tell you how they were used to solve the problem. Make sure you use both words and pictures.

## Talk with Children

○ Try to get in the habit of asking the children at the end of each day, *Did we solve any problems today?*

○ When a child describes a problem and a solution, ask, "How did you think of that solution?" This will help the child explain his or her thinking, a very important skill for both math and science.

○ Revisit your brainstorm list and discuss the many different solutions children suggested for just one problem. Use a sharing time or a circle time to talk to each other about problems and solutions.

## Observe Children

○ How do different children communicate their solutions to the problem? By acting them out? Talking about them?

○ Listen to the children's language. Are some children using the words *problem* and *solution*?

○ Some children will use single words or phrases, while others may use sentences to talk about the problems and solutions.

## EXTEND THE LEARNING

○ Make a game out of the question, "What would you do if...?" The children can take turns making up a problem while others try to come up with creative solutions to the problem. Here are some examples:
*What would you do if it's time to walk the dog and you can't find the leash?*
*What would you do if you were thirsty and the only cup you could find was leaky?*
Brainstorm all the possible solutions with the children. Be sure every child has a chance to suggest a problem and offer solutions. Write down the brainstorm list so the children can see their words. Remember, in a brainstorming session every answer is a good answer!

## CONNECT WITH FAMILIES

○ Display your data and children's drawings.
○ Post the following on your bulletin board:

### What Would You Do If...?

In this investigation we brainstormed many solutions to a problem, "How to get across hot sand without burning your feet," and then we acted out our solutions. First we used a beach towel and then we used a box, a jump rope, and a wooden spoon to solve the same problem. We also collected data on our investigation. We learned a lot thinking and talking about problems and their solutions, and we also learned that a single problem can have many solutions. We practiced:

• Using vocabulary words like *problem* and *solution*,

• Solving problems creatively, and

• Collecting data.

# INVESTIGATION: HOW DOES IT HELP US?

In this investigation, children examine and discuss everyday objects that help solve problems. They also discuss other creative ways to solve problems.

## WHAT'S NEEDED

chart paper or poster board

markers

objects that children are familiar with that could help solve a problem, such as a
bucket, paper bag, an adhesive bandage, pillow, potato masher, shoe, mitten,
colander, whisk broom, or a towel

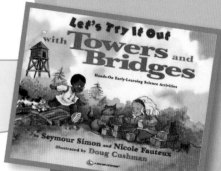

A book such as *Let's Try it Out with Towers and Bridges* by Seymour Simon is a great book to read while you do this investigation with the children.

## THINGS TO CONSIDER

Be sure you know what problem each of the objects is meant to solve.

## KEY SCIENCE STANDARDS CHILDREN PRACTICE

**Design Technology:** asking how we can use technology and simple devices to solve problems

**Science as Inquiry:** asking scientific questions about objects and what they can be used for

**Science as Inquiry:** collecting and using data to think about problems and solutions

**Science as Inquiry:** communicating ideas about problem solving

## STEP BY STEP

1. Show the children an object such as an adhesive bandage. Talk about how it was designed to help us solve a problem. Ask the children what problem a bandage was designed to solve.

2. Encourage the children to look carefully at the bandage and talk about the things they notice: it has adhesive; it has a pad; it's a rectangle. Ask the children if they can think of other uses for the bandage. Here are some examples: A bandage could be used to hang something on the wall, fix a hole in the window, or fix your glasses.

3. Continue this investigation using other objects, such as a shoe, a bucket, or any object from your collection. Encourage the children to select an object, tell what problem it was invented to solve, and come up with other uses for the object.

4. Create a chart. In one column, write the name of the item. In a second column, have the children draw an illustration of the object. In a third column, write the problem that the item solves. In a fourth column, write the children's ideas for other problems the item could solve.

### Talk with Children

○ Some children may have very creative but not practical ideas for how to use the objects. Be sure to let them know that when you are doing this kind of creative brainstorming there are no wrong answers. Praise their creative thinking.

### Observe Children

○ Listen for language development throughout the activity. Which children introduce words to others?
○ Listen to the children's conversations and see if there are words that you can help them use again.
○ Which children have creative ideas for the use of an object?
○ Notice how the children interact with an object. Are they curious about small details such as shape or design?

## EXTEND THE LEARNING

○ Talk with the children about inventions. Explain that inventions are things that people have created to solve a problem. Brainstorm a list of inventions. Let the children come up with this list on their own. Beginning with one invention, engage the children in a conversation about one of the inventions.

For example, about cars:

*How would we get from one place to another if we didn't have cars? How would we visit friends?*

*Go on a trip? Go shopping?*

Or about bridges:

*How could we get across the water if there were no bridge?*

In your everyday activities, help the children find and name inventions. Add these to your list of inventions.

## CONNECT WITH FAMILIES

○ Display one of the objects you discussed and the list of what the children said about the object, along with charts, drawings, or pictures.

○ Post the following:

### How Does It Help Us?

In this investigation we examined a collection of everyday objects that are used to help us solve problems. In our discussion we talked about what the objects are used for and we brainstormed other ways the object could be used. During this investigation we practiced:

• Thinking about how technology can be used to help solve problems and improve everyday life, and

• Problem solving with creative thinking.

# INVESTIGATION: BUILDING WITH BLOCKS

Children explore shapes and design while building with blocks.

## WHAT'S NEEDED

plastic, cardboard, or wooden blocks

Read books such as *The Three Little Pigs* by Paul Galdone or *The Three Little Javelinas* by Susan Lowell as you do this investigation with the children.

## THINGS TO CONSIDER

○ Have the children built with blocks before? Give the children plenty of time to play with the blocks before they start building. Let the children be the builders with occasional questions and comments from you.

## KEY MATH STANDARDS CHILDREN PRACTICE

**Communicating:** talking about the shapes, sizes, and number of blocks used

**Geometry and Spatial Sense:** combining shapes to make new shapes

**Problem Solving:** making the structures balance through counting and trial and error

## KEY SCIENCE STANDARDS CHILDREN PRACTICE

**Design Technology:** noticing problems and coming up with possible design changes

**Physical Science:** exploring building materials

**Science as Inquiry:** asking questions such as "What if...?," "How many...?," and "What's that...?"

**Science as Inquiry:** designing and making models

**Science as Inquiry:** recognizing patterns and relationships by talking about the blocks and their structures

Measuring, estimating, and comparing are some of the math and science skills children practice when they explore and build with blocks.

○ How many blocks tall can I make this?

○ Which tower is the tallest? Which is the shortest?

○ Is the house for the dog taller or shorter than the house for the giraffe?

○ Will I need more or fewer straws for this bridge?

○ How long is your bridge?

○ Which bridge will hold the most pennies?

○ Let's measure our house with paper clips. How many paper clips tall is your house? Is it taller than mine?

## STEP BY STEP

1. Ask the children what they would like to build with the blocks. The children will have many ideas of what they would like to build. Talk with the children about their ideas. When the children talk with you about what they want to build they are actually beginning to design the building.

2. Allow the children plenty of time to build. Encourage the children to talk about what's next as they place blocks on their structures. When they've finished with their buildings, encourage them to talk about their constructions with the group.
   *Does the shape of a block make any difference in building? Which shapes are best for walls? Which are best for corners? For openings?*
   *What happens when the structure gets really tall?*
   *What do you think is the most important block in a building? Why?*

3. Label the buildings. Use the exact words the children used to design their buildings and the words the children used while building. Be sure to include who the builder was on each label. Invite families to look at all the buildings.

### Talk with Children

○ Talk about how the children might use blocks to make their buildings sturdy or tall. Are some blocks better than others for a particular part of the structure?

○ Use the language of math and science: positional and comparative words; counting and number words; and words about colors, shape, and size.

○ Make connections between what the children build and buildings in books and the real world:
   *That looks like the firehouse next door.*
   *That's like the Three Bears' house.*
   *Is that an apartment house?*

○ Ask open-ended questions:
   *What if you used a square block there?*
   *What would happen if you used a differently shaped block here?*
   *Why did you use larger blocks at the bottom of the structure?*
   *How could you make the building stronger?*

### Observe Children

○ Which children build their own designs?

○ Which children try to make their building look like a picture or building they've seen?

○ Do the children notice and talk about the patterns of the blocks in their buildings? Do they notice and talk about the relationships between and among blocks?

○ Do you see the children using two small blocks to fill a large space?

○ Do the children use math and science language as they talk about their buildings?

○ Do some children like to build by themselves? Do others enjoy working with a group?

## EXTEND THE LEARNING: COPY MY DESIGN

Children communicate placement and names of blocks and follow directions.

### WHAT'S NEEDED

sets of solid building blocks

### STEP BY STEP

1. Put out the building blocks. Build a simple structure of three blocks and describe it as you add pieces. When you have finished, ask the children to make the same structure. (The colors might not be the same depending on how many children there are and how many blocks you have available.)

2. In pairs, have the children take turns being the designer and the builder. One child builds a simple structure of three to five blocks and the other child then builds the same structure. Encourage the children to practice describing their structures with names of shapes and positions. For example:
   *I built a house. The base is a square cube with a triangle roof on top.*

3. Try this more challenging activity. Stand a book or a folder in front of where you are building to hide your structure from view. Build a structure and describe it as you build. For example:
   *First I put down a rectangle block with a long side touching the table. Next I place a cylinder on end in the middle of the rectangle. Third I put a small triangle prism on top of the cylinder.*

Challenge the children to build the same structure without seeing it, using only the verbal directions. This can be much more difficult than using our eyes to see and copy a structure. Describing how to build a structure requires use of specific vocabulary of shapes and positions.

## EXTEND THE LEARNING: BUILDING TOWERS

Children combine and balance shapes while they build towers.

### WHAT'S NEEDED

camera (optional)
drawing materials
sets of the solid building blocks

### STEP BY STEP

1. Talk with the children about building towers.
   *What shapes can we use to make a strong base?*
2. Encourage the children to work together in small groups to build towers.
3. While children are building, observe and ask questions.
   *How did you keep the tower from falling down? What shapes did you use for the base? What do you think will happen if….? How many blocks tall is your tower? Which shape did you use the most? How can we find out if the tower is strong?*
4. Measure your towers with standard or nonstandard units and make a chart to display.

5. Have the children make drawings of the towers to take home. You can also take photos to make a display of the towers.

| Group | # of Shoelaces | # of Plastic Spoons | Inches |
|---|---|---|---|
| Group #1 | 1 | 7½ | 38 |
| Group #2 | 1½ | 11½ | 57 |
| Group #3 | ½ | 3¾ | 19 |

## EXTEND THE LEARNING: BUILDING BRIDGES
Children experiment with building bridges.

## WHAT'S NEEDED
bridge-building materials, such as solid blocks, paper cups, books, paper, straws, and tape
drawings or photos of bridges
small figures, animals, or cars to test the strength of the bridges

When you build, read a book such as *Let's Try it Out with Towers and Bridges* by Seymour Simon.

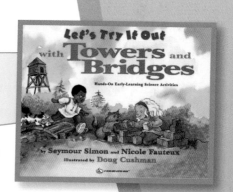

## STEP BY STEP
1. Display some drawings or photos of real bridges. Ask:
   *Where do we use bridges? What shapes do you see in the bridges?*
A bridge can be as simple as a log across a stream or as complex as the interconnected towers and cables of the Golden Gate Bridge.
2. Challenge the children to build a bridge by placing a sheet of paper between two stacks of blocks, paper cups, or books.
3. Test the bridge with small figures. Ask:
   *Can the people cross the bridge? Can you make the bridge stronger?*
Encourage the children to arch, fold, or pleat the paper and test the bridge again.

*How can we make the bridge even stronger?*
*What materials might we use?*

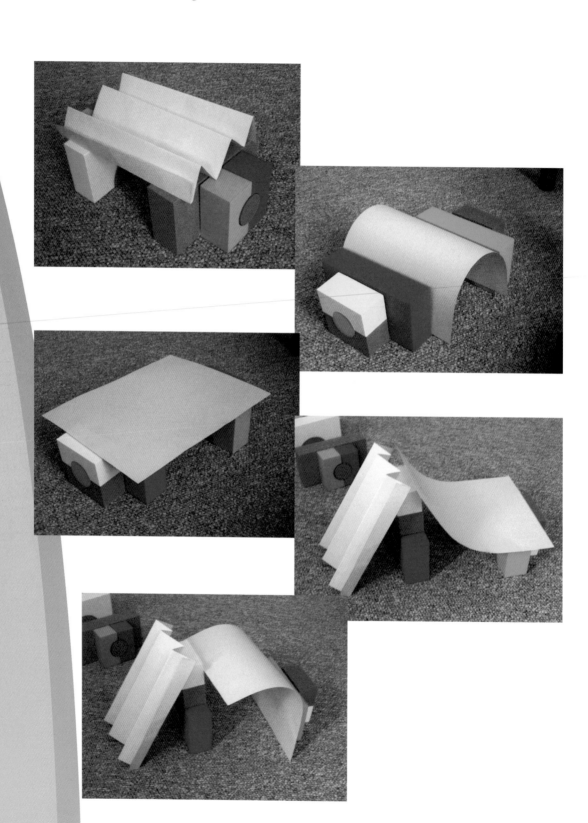

MATH AND SCIENCE INVESTIGATIONS

## EXTEND THE LEARNING: BUILDING ENCLOSED STRUCTURES

Children design and build a structure for a specific purpose.

## WHAT'S NEEDED

building materials, such as sets of solid building blocks, foam shapes, plastic cups, film canisters, paper towel tubes, and pieces of cardboard

camera (optional)

nonstandard measuring tools, such as paper clips, blocks, books, and so on

paper and markers

tape or glue

## STEP BY STEP

1. Invite the children to build a structure for a specific purpose, such as a garage for a truck, a house for a horse, and so on.
2. While the children are building, observe, ask questions, and find out the story of the children's structures.

   *Tell me about your structure. Why are you building a house for a horse?*
3. Talk about design aspects and material choices

   *Is the building wide enough for the truck?*

   *I wonder how the people will get into the house.*

   *How did you arrange the cups to make them stand up?*
4. Use a nonstandard measuring tool to make comparisons among the structures.
5. Take photos to make a display of the structures. The children can dictate descriptions of the structures to add to the photos.

## CONNECT WITH FAMILIES

Display the block structures or photographs of them along with the following information:

### Building with Blocks

We've been building with blocks. We experimented with blocks of different sizes and shapes. Some of our buildings were imaginative, and others were like the buildings in our neighborhood. While we were building we practiced:

• Using math and science vocabulary: *over, near, bigger than, smaller than, shorter than, same as;*

• Asking questions such as "What if I use two blocks here instead of one?" or "How many blocks do I need to make the sides balance?";

• Using numbers and counting by adding "one more" and taking away or adding blocks;

• Looking at and talking about the patterns and relationships in our structures;

• Making changes in our buildings when there was a design problem.

# INVESTIGATION: ALUMINUM FOIL BOATS

In this investigation, children form aluminum foil into boat shapes and experiment with how to make the boats float and carry objects.

## WHAT'S NEEDED

large plastic dishpan filled with water for each small group

objects to be used as passengers or cargo in the boats (pennies, washers, paper clips, toy animals)

pictures of boats (optional)

three or four pieces of aluminum foil for each child (the pieces can be any shape and size but should be at least 6" x 6")

Read a book such as *Who Sank the Boat?* by Pamela Allen as you do this investigation with the children.

## THINGS TO CONSIDER

O Many children will be interested in doing this investigation again and again to try different boat designs.

O Tell families about this investigation ahead of time so the children can bring in an extra shirt.

## KEY MATH STANDARDS CHILDREN PRACTICE

**Geometry and Spatial Sense:** using words to describe where objects are placed in the boat

**Numbers and Operations:** counting and comparing the number of objects going into the boat

## KEY SCIENCE STANDARDS CHILDREN PRACTICE

**Physical Science:** experimenting with water and exploring the physical properties of water and aluminum foil

**Science as Inquiry:** asking scientific questions such as "What would happen if my boat was made this way?" or "I wonder why that happened?"

**Science as Inquiry:** predicting what will happen with a particular boat, and then refining the design

## STEP BY STEP

1. Show the children a flat sheet of foil. Discuss together the many ways the foil can be shaped into boats. Together, make several different boats and test them in the water.

2. Give each child a piece of foil to use to make a boat. The children can test the boats in the dishpans filled with water. (Almost any shape with the sides folded up will float, so do not expect to see all the designs look like traditional boats.) Some children may want to look at pictures of boats for ideas.

3. Give each child several objects ("passengers" or "cargo") to put in his or her boat. Some children may want to count how many objects their boat can carry.
   **Note**: If you're making comparisons between what two boats will hold, the types of objects placed in the boats must be identical.
4. Talk with the children about their boats and what they noticed about what happened when they put "passengers" in the boat.
5. Look at the children's boats and have a conversation about boat design. Which shapes did the children think made the best boats? Which held the most objects?
6. Repeat this investigation and test the group's ideas.

### Talk with Children

O As the children experiment with their boats, ask questions such as:
   *What happens when you add more objects to your boat?*
   *What do you notice about how you place objects in your boat?*
   *How many objects does your boat hold? If a boat sinks, try again.*
   *If you change the shape of the boat, can it carry more weight?*

### Observe Children

O Notice how the children explore different possibilities while experimenting with the boats.
O Do the same children always create the same boat?
O Are there some children who change the design of their boat over and over? What are their reasons for changing a design?
O Listen carefully to the children's words during this activity. Some children will talk as they create their boats.
O What kinds of questions are the children asking?
O Are the children giving explanations for what happens?
   *(I think it sank because I tried to put too many plastic animals in it.)*

## EXTEND THE LEARNING

O For children who want to continue building and testing boats, set up a place where a dishpan of water, some sheets of foil, and some objects are available. The children can continue to design boats and experiment with putting objects in their boat to act out the story of *Who Sank the Boat?* and test boat designs.

## CONNECT WITH FAMILIES

○ Display the collection of children's boats.

○ Post the following on your bulletin board:

### Aluminum Foil Boats

We made boats out of aluminum foil and then experimented to find out how many objects each boat could hold before it sank. Then we improved our boat designs and tried again. By building and testing boats we practiced:

• Using our design skills,

• Counting the objects each boat holds,

• Predicting which boat will hold more and testing our predictions, and

• Using positional words to describe where we placed objects in the boats.

# INVESTIGATION: BOATS FROM EVERYDAY OBJECTS

In this investigation, children use various materials to make boats and expand their experience with designing and testing.

## WHAT'S NEEDED

boat-building materials such as Styrofoam meat trays, milk cartons, paper and plastic cups, craft sticks, large plastic lids from cottage cheese or deli containers, margarine tubs, string, and tape

chart paper and marker, string, or yarn to make circles on the floor

collection of books about boats or pictures of different types of boats

objects for cargo

plastic dishpans

> Books about boats such as *Boats: Speeding! Sailing! Cruising!* by Patricia Hubbell or *Who Sank the Boat?* by Pamela Allen are excellent to read with the children as you do this investigation.

## THINGS TO CONSIDER

O What are some of the things the children did with aluminum foil boats?

## KEY MATH STANDARDS CHILDREN PRACTICE

**Geometry and Spatial Sense:** describing in detail how each boat moves in the water or sinks

## KEY SCIENCE STANDARDS CHILDREN PRACTICE

**Design Technology:** responding to What if...? questions

**Design Technology:** using varied materials to build and invent

**Physical Science:** learning about solids in water

**Science as Inquiry:** experimenting with different materials, designing different boats, and testing their boats in the water

**Science as Inquiry:** recognizing relationships between materials used and successful boats

**Science as Inquiry:** sorting the boats by building materials

## STEP BY STEP

1. Engage the children in a conversation about what they experienced in the Aluminum Foil Boats investigation.
   *What did they learn about making boats? How did they shape the foil into a boat? What shapes were successful at carrying passengers or cargo?*

2. Show the children pictures of boats and discuss with them the similarities and differences between and among boats.

3. Talk about designing a boat from the displayed materials. Have the children make observations about the boat-building materials, talking about size, shape, and weight.

4. Allow the children to choose from the supplies and make a boat. They may want to tape on a stick and attach a sail, some may want to make a "motor" from Legos, others may want to make oars like the boat in *Who Sank the Boat?*

5. Allow plenty of time for the children to experiment with their boats in the water.

6. Once the children have a boat that floats, encourage the children to see if the boat will carry any cargo by adding weights or objects.

7. After the children have designed, tested, and redesigned their boats, bring the children together to talk about experiences. Have two circles on the floor or on chart paper and have the children sort the materials or boats into groups: great material for a boat, not-so-great material for a boat, carried cargo, didn't carry cargo, and so on.

## Talk with Children

○ As you encourage the children to talk about their observations encourage them to think about several solutions to the problems they encounter. For example, if the boat tilts or turns upside down you might ask:

*Does the boat tilt on the same side each time?*

*Does it flip over slowly or quickly?*

*What are some ways you could make the boat tilt in the opposite direction?*

*Do some materials balance better than others? How are the materials alike or different? Do they have the same shape?*

○ If two children are grappling with the same problem, suggest they talk together.

## Observe Children

○ Listen for talk about similar experiences. For example, "I remember the flat aluminum boat stayed up better than the log shape" or "What would Lottie do?"

○ Are the children using positional words such as *over, under,* and *around*? Are the children using comparative language such as *heavier than, longer than,* and *bigger than*?

○ Notice how the children work with the materials.

○ Which children try the same thing over and over? Which children make boats that have symmetry and balance?

## EXTEND THE LEARNING: RECYCLED BUILDING

Try building with recycled materials!

## WHAT'S NEEDED

camera

paper

recycled/found materials such as shoeboxes, paper towel tubes, paper cups, straws,
      cereal boxes, clean yogurt containers and lids, and so on

scissors

tape and glue

## STEP BY STEP

1. Display the variety of materials and talk about them. Compare and discuss the
   attributes of each material such as strength, flexibility, and weight.
2. Ask the children what they would like to build. Ideas might include a fire truck,
   a garage, or a house for a small toy. Possibilities are unlimited!
3. Allow the children time to explore the materials and test some ideas. It will be
   helpful to have extra adult helpers for the construction part when materials get
   taped or glued together.
4. Encourage the children to talk about what they have done:
   *Tell me about your project. Why did you choose this material to build your _____?*
5. Take photos of the children as they work and of the finished projects.

## CONNECT WITH FAMILIES

○ Display examples of the children's boats, photographs of the investigation, and
   everyday objects that families can take home and use to make boats.
○ Post the following on your bulletin board:

### Boats from Everyday Objects

We have been using everyday materials to make boats. This involves predicting
which materials and designs will work well and testing our predictions. When we
made boats we practiced:

• Making boats that would float,

• Predicting and testing boats, and

• Experimenting with different materials.

# INVESTIGATION: CREATING LETTERS

In this investigation children will experiment with ways to construct the letters of the alphabet using various materials.

## WHAT'S NEEDED

variety of materials, including items that can bend or be shaped into letters, such as feathers, craft sticks, chenille sticks, playdough, toothpicks, and recycled materials such as egg cartons, toilet paper rolls, and empty boxes.

Read a book such as *Albert's Alphabet* by Leslie Tryon as you do this investigation with the children.

## THINGS TO CONSIDER

○ The ages of your group: some children may be able to make the first letter or some of the letters in their own names; others will be able to make any letter of the alphabet.

○ If you do not have an alphabet posted, write out the alphabet in simple block letters so that the children can look at the letters as they work.

○ This investigation is about using materials in different ways. Encourage the children to use familiar materials in new ways.

## KEY MATH STANDARDS CHILDREN PRACTICE

**Geometry and Spatial Sense:** combining shapes to make letters

## KEY SCIENCE STANDARD CHILDREN PRACTICE

**Physical Science:** learning about the properties of objects, i.e., some materials are rigid and some are flexible

**Science as Inquiry:** communicating results

**Science as Inquiry:** designing and making models of letters

**Science as Inquiry:** experimenting with materials

## STEP BY STEP

1. Examine and talk about the materials together. Which would be best for making the letter "O"? Why? Which would be best for making the letter "H"?

2. Have every child find and use materials to make the first letter of the alphabet, "A." Talk with the children about the ways they made "A."

3. If you have a large group of children, you can give a small group an "assignment" of several letters written on a piece of paper. Remind the children that they'll want to test the different materials to see which is best for each letter.

4. Help the children complete the alphabet and arrange the letters in the correct order. If you have a camera, photograph the alphabet.

### Talk with Children

○ Help the children become aware of the distinctiveness of each letter of the alphabet and of the materials for reproducing the letters. You might say:
*A has straight sides. Can you find something straight to be the side of A?*
*B has many curves. What could we use? Could we use something that bends, or something flexible? Does anyone know what* flexible *means?*

### Observe Children

○ Which children see many possibilities for each material? Which children see a material as having only one use?

○ How much planning are the children doing when they make the letters? Do some children work by trial and error with no planning? Look for:
Children saving materials for a future letter
Children making space for a letter

○ Do children recognize the letters in their names?

## EXTEND THE LEARNING

○ Another way to make the alphabet is to make the shape of letters out of children's bodies. Since this takes more than one child, it will require lots of teamwork. Take photos if you can.

## CONNECT WITH FAMILIES

Display photographs and/or the letters you made, along with the following:

**Creating Letters**

We challenged ourselves to build the alphabet with many different materials. When we did this we practiced:

• Solving problems creatively by using materials in different ways,

• Planning where each letter would go, and

• Engineering skills by understanding what materials are useful for different applications.

MATH AND SCIENCE INVESTIGATIONS

# Bibliography

This Bibliography contains picture books recommended for the math and science themes addressed in this manual. Our online database is updated frequently as new books are published. Search www.mothergooseprograms.org to find the newest titles.

## Measurement

Goldstone, B. 2010. *Great Estimations*. New York: Square Fish.
If someone handed you a big bowl of jelly beans, how would you figure out how many there are? You could count them, one by one, or you could estimate. This unique book will show you how to train your eyes and your mind to make really great estimations.

Hightower, S. 1997. *Twelve Snails to One Lizard*. New York: Simon & Schuster.
A silly story about inches, feet, and yards.

Jenkins, S. 2004. *Actual Size*. Boston: Houghton Mifflin Harcourt.
How big is a crocodile? Can you imagine a two-foot-long tongue? Sometimes facts and figures don't tell the whole story. Sometimes you need to see things for yourself— at their actual size.

Jenkins, S. 1997. *Biggest, Strongest, Fastest*. Boston: Houghton Mifflin Harcourt.
An informative introduction to the "world records" held by fourteen members of the animal kingdom.

Leedy, L. 2000. *Measuring Penny*. New York: Henry Holt.
For homework, Lisa measures her dog, Penny. She uses standard and nonstandard measures.

Lionni, L. 2010. *Inch by Inch*. New York: Knopf.
A story of an inchworm who measures his way out of being eaten by a bird.

Myller, R. 1990. *How Big Is a Foot?* New York: Random House.
The king wants to give the queen something special for her birthday. The queen has everything, everything except a bed. The trouble is that no one in the kingdom knows the answer to a very important question: How big is a bed? (Here's the catch: beds had not yet been invented.)

Tompert, A. 1996. *Just a Little Bit*. Boston: Sandpiper.
When Elephant and Mouse try to play on a seesaw, they need help from a vast number of animal friends to balance the scales.

## More Than Counting

Anno, Mitsumasa. 1977. *Anno's Counting Book*. New York: HarperCollins.
Introduces counting and number systems by showing mathematical relationships in nature.

Bang, M. 1991. *Ten, Nine, Eight*. New York: HarperCollins.
A counting lullaby showing the room of a little girl going to bed.

Chae, I. 2008. *How Do You Count a Dozen Ducklings?* Park Ridge, IL: Whitman.
A mama duck with a dozen eggs has to do a lot of counting! Mama counts her ducklings one by one as they hatch, but soon she finds clever new ways to count to twelve—by twos, threes, fours, and sixes! But how many ducklings will it take to trick the hungry wolf who is counting on them for lunch?

Christelow, E. 1990. *Five Little Monkeys Jumping on the Bed*. New York: Scholastic.
As soon as they say good night to Mama, the five little monkeys start to jump on their bed. But trouble lies ahead.

Hines, A.G. 2008. *1, 2, Buckle My Shoe*. Boston: Harcourt.
Take cloth and buttons and thread. Add a classic nursery rhyme and a counting game. Stitch them together and what do you have? A patchwork of numbers and fun!

Hutchins, P. 1986. *The Doorbell Rang*. New York: HarperCollins.
Ma gives Sam and Victoria a dozen cookies to share—plenty for two children. But then, the doorbell rings and rings and rings as more children arrive to share the cookies. Finally, each child has just one cookie. And then...what happens next?

Merriam, E. 1996. *12 Ways to Get to 11*. New York: Aladdin.
Go on an adventure with this innovative counting book.

Pinczes, E. 1993. *One Hundred Hungry Ants*. Boston: Houghton.
One hundred ants march toward a picnic and the littlest ant decides he'd like to step up the pace.

Rathmann, P. 1998. *10 Minutes till Bedtime*. New York: Penguin.
What the humans at 1 Hoppin Place don't know is that their cherished family pet hamster has advertised on the Web (www.hamstertours.com) for a "10-Minute Bedtime Tour," and the hordes have only just begun to descend.

Root, P. 2001. *One Duck Stuck*. Somerville, MA: Candlewick.
Different marshland creatures offer to help one duck stuck in the muck.

Walton, R. 1993. *How Many, How Many, How Many*. Somerville, MA: Candlewick.
The reader counts from one to twelve while guessing the answers to questions about nursery rhymes, names of the seasons, players on a football team, and other basic information.

Young, E. 2002. *Seven Blind Mice*. London: Puffin.
One by one, seven blind mice investigate the strange Something by the pond. What is it?

## Out and About

Asch, F. 1985. *Moonbear's Shadow*. New York: Aladdin.
A story of a bear and his shadow and how they work things out.

Branley, F. 1997. *Down Comes the Rain*. New York: HarperCollins.
The ups and downpours of the water cycle.

Brenner, B. 2004. *One Small Place in a Tree*. New York: HarperCollins.
A glimpse of nature in action is offered by zeroing in on "one small place" teeming with living things.

Bulla, C. R. 1994. *What Makes a Shadow?* New York: HarperCollins.
This book tells us how shadows are made and then encourages readers to look for shadows in a variety of places.

Crews, N. 1995. *One Hot Summer Day*. New York: Greenwillow.
Relates a child's activities in the heat of a summer day punctuated by a thunderstorm.

DeWitt, L. 1993. *What Will the Weather Be?* New York: HarperCollins.
Will it be warm or cold? Should we wear shorts or pants? Shoe or boots? Find out why the weather is so difficult to predict.

Dorros, A. 1990. *Feel the Wind.* New York: HarperCollins.
All about wind—what causes it and how it affects our environment. Includes instructions for making a weathervane.

Ehlert, L. 1991. *Red Leaf, Yellow Leaf*. San Diego: Harcourt.
Introduction to the life of a tree.

Gibbons, G. 2002. *Tell Me, Tree*. Boston: Little, Brown.
Discusses parts of the tree and their functions, types of fruits and seeds, kinds of bark, and uses for trees.

Gibbons, G. 1992. *Weather Words and What They Mean*. New York: Holiday House.
Temperature, air pressure, moisture, and wind are broadly defined and illustrated in Gibbons' explanations of sometimes misunderstood weather terms. One page of curious weather facts concludes the book.

Hesse, K. 1999. *Come On, Rain*. New York: Scholastic.
A young girl waits for the rain to bring respite from summer heat.

Hest, A. 1995. *In the Rain with Baby Duck*. Cambridge, MA: Candlewick.
Mother Duck is upset because Baby Duck hates the rain, but Grampa Duck reminds Mother that once she had to have an umbrella and little boots too.

Hoban, T. 1990. *Shadows and Reflections*. New York: Greenwillow.
Photographs without text feature shadows and reflections of objects, animals, and people.

Lauber, P. 1994. *Be a Friend to Trees*. New York: HarperCollins.
A lot of information is conveyed in a simple text with clear line-and-watercolor illustrations as the author shows that we cannot live without trees.

Pfeffer, W. 1997. *A Log's Life*. New York: Simon & Schuster.
This introduction to the life cycle of a tree presents the complex cast of characters residing in or on the living tree as well as the decomposing log from woodpeckers, squirrels, and porcupines to carpenter ants, millipedes, slugs, and fungi.

Shulevitz, U. 1998. *Snow*. New York: Frances Foster.
As snowflakes slowly come down, one by one, people in the city ignore them, and only a boy and his dog think that the snowfall will amount to anything.

Tompert, A. 1991. *Nothing Sticks Like a Shadow*. Boston: Houghton Mifflin.
To win a bet with Woodchuck, Rabbit tries to get rid of his shadow.

## Shapes and Spaces

Dodds, D.A. 1994. *The Shape of Things*. Somerville, MA: Candlewick.
Simple rhymes and bold illustrations help youngsters learn to see and, eventually, to draw the world around them.

Gibbons, G. 2004. *The Quilting Bee*. New York: HarperCollins.
A "quilting circle" consisting of adults and two child helpers plan a new quilt to display at the county fair. Readers learn how quilts are made and discover their fascinating history as well as lots of fun facts.

Gravett, E. 2007. *Orange Pear Apple Bear*. New York: Simon & Schuster.
A plump bear adds a humorous touch to this charming book about shapes, colors, and sequence.

Hoban, T. 1986. *Shapes, Shapes, Shapes*. New York: Greenwillow.
A wordless picture book that encourages children to find shapes.

Micklethwait, L. 2004. *I Spy Shapes in Art*. New York: Greenwillow.
Presents shapes evident in paintings by such artists as Homer, O'Keefe, Klee, and Matisse.

Rau, D. 2002. *A Star in My Orange*. Brookfield, CT: Millbrook.
Rau looks to nature for inspiration and finds stars not just in the sky but in an orange half, a starfish, and a snowflake. She sees spirals in a seahorse, a ram's horns, and a seashell. A very simple yet effective book presenting fundamental forms that children can observe in nature.

Tompert, A. 1990. *Grandfather Tang's Story*. New York: Crown.
This original tangram tale is framed by the loving relationship between a grandfather and a granddaughter as they share the story under the shade of an old tree.

Walsh, E. 2007. *Mouse Shapes*. Orlando, FL: Harcourt.
What can you make with one oval, two circles, and eight triangles? Just ask three clever mice—who even find a funny way to trick a sneaky cat.

## Exploring Spaces (and Places!)

Chancellor, D. 2004. *Maps and Mapping*. New York: Kingfisher.
Introduces children to basic facts about maps—what they are, how they are made and used, and the symbols and projections found on them. Also includes several simple projects.

Fanelli, S. 1995. *My Map Book*. New York: HarperCollins.
A collection of maps provides views of the owner's bedroom, school, playground, and other realms farther away.

Hartman, G. 1993. *As the Crow Flies: A First Book of Maps*. New York: Aladdin.
An exploration of map skills following the paths of several animals.

Hutchins, P. 1968. *Rosie's Walk*. New York: Aladdin.
The fox is after Rosie, but Rosie doesn't know it. She leads him on a long walk, into one disaster after the other, each one more fun than the last.

Leedy, L. 2000. *Mapping Penny's World*. New York: Henry Holt.
A girl maps her bedroom and her dog Penny's world.

Penner, L.R.. 2000. *Where's That Bone?* Minneapolis, MN: Kane Press.
A young girl uses a map to keep track of where her dog buries his bones.

Schertle, A. 1995. *Down the Road*. Orlando, FL: Harcourt.
Hetty is very careful with the eggs she has bought on her very first trip to the store, but she runs into trouble when she stops to pick apples.

Stock, C. 1993. *Where Are You Going Manyoni?* New York: HarperCollins.
A child living near the Limpopo River in Zimbabwe encounters several wild animals on her long walk to school.

Sweeney, J. 1998. *Me on the Map*. New York: Dragonfly.
A young girl introduces the world of mapmaking. She begins with the floor plans of her room and house and then expands from home to street, to town, to state, to country, and finally to the world.

## What Comes Next?

Galdone, P. 1972. *The Three Bears*. New York: Clarion.
This and many of the classic folktales illustrate patterns in language and size.

Harris, T. 2000. *Pattern Fish*. Grand Ledge, MI: Millbrook.
A fun look at patterns.

Pfeffer, W. 1998. *Sounds All Around*. New York: HarperCollins.
Clap your hands, snap your fingers: You're making sounds. Find out how people and animals use different kinds of sounds to communicate.

Pinkney, B. 1997. *Max Found Two Sticks*. New York: Simon & Schuster.
Although he doesn't feel like talking, Max responds to questions by drumming on various objects.

Pluckrose, H.A. 1995. *Patterns*. San Francisco: Children's Press.
Large colorful photos of everyday things help reinforce the text in this fun, easy introduction to the concept of patterns.

Smalls, I. 1992. *Jonathan and His Mommy*. New York: Little, Brown.
As a mother and son explore their neighborhood, they try various ways of walking.

Swinburne, S. 2002. *Lots and Lots of Zebra Stripes*. Honesdale, PA: Boyds.
The author defines patterns as "lines and shapes that repeat" and finds these patterns everywhere.

MATH AND SCIENCE INVESTIGATIONS

## Growing and Changing

Aliki. 1993. *I'm Growing!* New York: HarperCollins.
With her trademark simple words and delightful pictures, Aliki explains how and why we grow. The discussion includes bones, muscles, teeth, plus internal organs.

Bishop, N. 2007. *Spiders*. New York: Scholastic.
Simple, engaging text conveys basic information about spiders as well as cool and quirky facts.

Doyle, M. 2002. *Jody's Beans*. Cambridge, MA: Candlewick.
Jody and her grandfather plant bean seeds together. He visits occasionally, but it's up to Jody to tend the beans.

Gibbons, G. 1993. *From Seed to Plant*. New York: Holiday House.
This is a simple introduction to how plants reproduce, discussing pollination, seed dispersal, and growth from seed to plant. A simple project—how to grow a bean plant—is included.

Gibbons, G. 1989. *Monarch Butterfly*. New York: Holiday House.
Describes the life cycle, body parts, and behavior of the monarch butterfly. Includes instructions on how to raise a monarch.

Hickman, P. 1999. *A New Frog*. Toronto; Buffalo, NY: Kids Can.
The life of a frog from conception to adulthood as seen by a little girl on her visits to the edge of a pond.

Hutchins, Pat. 1983. *You'll Soon Grow into Them, Titch*. New York: HarperCollins.
Titch is not the only person who is growing and changing in this book. While we watch Titch move from one set of hand-me-downs to another, in the background the plants and birds are growing, the seasons are changing, and Mom's knitting project is progressing.

Jarrett, C. 2008. *Arabella Miller's Tiny Caterpillar*. Cambridge, Mass.: Candlewick.
When Arabella Miller finds a tiny caterpillar, she brings him home and feeds him lots and lots of leaves.

Jordan, H. 1992. *How a Seed Grows*. New York: HarperCollins.
Uses observations of bean seeds planted in eggshells to demonstrate the growth of seeds into plants.

Krauss, R. 1973. *The Carrot Seed*. New York: HarperCollins.
A little boy plants a carrot seed. His mother, father and big brother agree that it won't come up but the little boy knows better.

Perkins, L. 1995. *Home Lovely*. New York: Greenwillow.
Tiffany transplants and cares for some seedlings. With help from a friendly postman, she makes a real garden.

Richards, J. 2006. *A Fruit Is a Suitcase for Seeds*. Brookfield, CT: First Avenue.
Richards's carefully worded information provides an excellent introduction to seeds, their purpose, and growth that should be easy for young children to grasp.

Rockwell, A. 2001. *Growing Like Me*. San Diego: Harcourt.
Explains how plants and animals of the meadow, woods, and pond grow and evolve, such as caterpillars changing into butterflies, eggs hatching into robins, and acorns becoming oaks.

Sklansky, A. 2005. *Where Do Chicks Come From?* New York: HarperCollins.
Children will be fascinated about the details of life inside an egg as we follow the development from its beginning as a "tiny white spot" inside the mother to 20 days later when the chick begins to breathe and make sounds.

Stevens, J. 1995. *Tops and Bottoms*. San Diego: Harcourt.
Hare turns his bad luck around by striking a clever deal with the rich and lazy bear down the road.

## Same and Different

Berkes, M. 2002. *Seashells by the Seashore*. Nevada City, CA: Dawn.
Sue walks the shore, collecting seashells for her grandmother's birthday.

Gans, R. 1997. *Let's Go Rock Collecting*. New York: HarperCollins.
Readers follow two rock hounds around the globe as they add to their collection.

Gibbons, G. 1982. *Tool Book*. New York: Holiday House.
This book shows tools used in building and describes what they are used for.

Hoban, T. 1984. *Is it Rough? Is it Smooth? Is it Shiny?* New York: Greenwillow.
Color photographs introduce objects of many different textures.

Jenkins, E. 2001. *Five Creatures*. New York: Frances Foster.
A girl describes the three humans and two cats that live in her house, and details some shared traits.

Jocelyn, M. 2004. *Hannah's Collections*. Toronto: Tundra.
Hannah has a challenge: which of her many collections should she choose to share with her class?

Nikola-Lisa, W. 1994. *Bein' with You This Way*. New York: Lee & Low.
A rap poem with rich, catchy phrases that celebrate diversity.

MATH AND SCIENCE INVESTIGATIONS

Pluckrose, H. 1995. *Sorting*. London: Watts.
Uses everyday objects to introduce the concept of sorting.

Reid, M. 1990. *The Button Box*. New York: Puffin.
A little boy explores his grandmother's button box.

## Making It Work

Burningham, J. 1995. *Mr. Gumpy's Outing*. New York: Holt.
Mr. Gumpy tries to teach his passengers the correct way to ride in a boat.

Hoberman, M. A. 1978. *A House Is a House for Me*. New York: Viking.
Lists in rhyme the dwellings of various animals and things.

Hubbell, P. 2009. *Boats: Speeding! Sailing! Cruising!* Tarrytown, NY: Cavendish.
Describes all kinds of boats and how they are used.

Hutchins, P. 1987. *Changes, Changes*. New York: Simon & Schuster.
Pat Hutchins shows, but does not tell, how blocks become whatever a child at play imagines.

Lindbergh, R. 1998. *Nobody Owns the Sky*. Cambridge, MA: Candlewick.
Bessie Coleman dreamed of becoming a pilot and she stuck with her dream until she made it come true.

Lowell, S. 1970. *The Three Little Javelinas*. Flagstaff, AZ: Northland.
This clever and humorous tale is sure to delight children of all ages, especially those familiar with the Southwest. Dressed in cowboy duds and prepared for life in the rugged dessert, these characters are more than any coyote bargained for.

Rockwell, A. 1993. *Boats*. New York: Puffin.
All about boats: freighters, steamers, ocean liners, rowboats, barges and toy boats.

Tryon, L. 1991. *Albert's Alphabet*. New York: Simon & Schuster.
Clever Albert uses all the supplies in his workshop to build an alphabet for the school playground.